Locking Loops

THERESA PULIDO

UNIQUE LOCKER HOOKING HANDCRAFTS
TO GIVE AND WEAR

KRAUSE PUBLICATIONS
CINCINNATI, OHIO

www.fwmedia.com

15 14 13 12 11   5 4 3 2 1

DISTRIBUTED IN CANADA BY FRASER DIRECT
100 Armstrong Avenue
Georgetown, ON, Canada L7G 5S4
Tel: (905) 877-4411

DISTRIBUTED IN THE U.K. AND EUROPE BY F&W MEDIA
INTERNATIONAL
Brunel House, Newton Abbot, Devon, TQ12 4PU, England
Tel: (+44) 1626 323200, Fax: (+44) 1626 323319
Email:enquiries@fwmedia.com

DISTRIBUTED IN AUSTRALIA BY CAPRICORN LINK
P.O. Box 704, S. Windsor NSW, 2756 Australia
Tel: (02) 4577-3555

SRN: Y1751
ISBN-13: 9781440215810

Edited by Jennifer Claydon
Designed by Marissa Bowers
Production coordinated by Greg Nock
Photography by Christine Polomsky, Ric Deliantoni and
douglasthompsonphoto.com
Styling by Lauren Emmerling and Beatriz Posada
F+W Media, Inc. would like to thank Scot Andrews and
Beatriz Posada for generously sharing the beautiful location
shown in this book.

METRIC CONVERSION CHART

Measurements have been given in Imperial inches with metric conversion in brackets—use one or the other as they are not interchangeable. The most accurate results will be obtained using inches.

TO CONVERT	TO	MULTIPLY BY
Inches	Centimeters	2.54
Centimeters	Inches	0.4
Feet	Centimeters	30.5
Centimeters	Feet	0.03
Yards	Meters	0.9
Meters	Yards	1.1

DEDICATION

This book is dedicated to all artisan crafters and artists who have made it their mission to share their creativity with others. Inspiration is a wonderful gift.

ACKNOWLEDGMENTS

I feel truly blessed to be surrounded by such a diverse group of inspirational people—friends and fellow crafters with their own unique sense of creativity—many of them right in my neighborhood and some whom I have connected with in other countries. Each is unique in what they bring to their craft, their living spaces and what they share with others, whether it's an unusual design, color choice, piece of art, new cooking recipe or just a new plant they've added to their gardens. I am eternally thankful for their inspiration. I have also met so many wonderful artisans and craft vendors that are producing amazing products. Whether it's hand-dyed silks and batik fabrics, natural textiles, fabulous luminescent fabric paints, vintage accents, beads or other collectibles, I am always in awe and can't wait to try a new find or unveil the next discovery. And I have to mention, in this day and age of diminishing customer service quality, I have found arts and crafts vendors that offer exceptional customer service. What a great experience to get personal customer support. I'd like to mention a few exceptional cases: Artemis, Inc., distributors of Hanah Silk products; Nina Designs; Rupert, Gibbon & Spider, makers of Jacquard Products; Mary Jo Hiney Designs; and Princess Mirah Design/Bali Fabrics.

I truly appreciate the support of my publisher, F+W Media, Inc., and editor Jenni Claydon. I also want to thank readers of my first book, *Hook, Loop & Lock*, who have given me so much invaluable feedback and have become true locker hooking enthusiasts. Please continue to forward your questions and feedback. You provide great company and make me feel just a tad bit less crazy for my addiction to this craft. I want to include a special "Thank you!" to Scot Andews and Beatriz Posada for their invaluable support. And, I couldn't do any of this without the support of my husband, Chris. He even helped me finish one of the projects for this book!

ABOUT THE AUTHOR

Driven by her passion for color and design, Theresa Pulido has always sought out unique objects that feature compelling designs, whether found in nature or crafted by hand. Theresa applies this passion to her own surroundings and handmade creations. She's the author of *Hook, Loop & Lock*, her first book on locker hooking, and spends her time promoting the craft through her business, Color Crazy, and through various presentations, workshops and videos. After a twenty-year career in high tech, Theresa decided to pursue a more creative track that taps her passion for color and anything that is handcrafted. Theresa is always developing new designs and finding unique ways to create with fabric, fiber and mixed media. She also enjoys gardening, cooking, photography and scouting for new handcrafted products and vintage accents. To learn more about Theresa's designs and patterns, visit colorcrazy.com and be sure to check out the gallery.

Table of Contents

Introduction

After writing my first book, *Hook, Loop & Lock*, I thought I might have said everything I have to say about locker hooking. However, because of many requests from readers, and my own attraction (or, I should say, addiction) to this wonderful craft, I was soon brimming with ideas for a second book. The reason for my love of locker hooking is quite simple: Unlike other rug-making or needlecraft techniques, locker hooking allows you to create shapes and assemble pieces together in ways that make the creative possibilities really quite endless. You can locker hook almost any shape you want as long as you use a simple technique to secure your edges. Different shapes can be used as embellishments, ornaments, coasters, totebags, mats, wall hangings and even jewelry. In this book I introduce unique new designs for making tote bags and baskets, bracelets, pins and a lovely necklace design. Using the techniques in Chapter One, you can pair your imagination with great materials and see wonderful projects unfold. I'm excited to share (and hopefully pass on) my passion for this craft with you!

There is another reason for my locker hooking loyalty. Locker hooking, like many other crafts, is a meditative outlet that allows me to lose myself in creativity; I can express myself with a variety of fibers and textures. It can be very stress relieving! You can experience this whether you make a tiny project like a floral accent or something larger like a rug.

The projects in this book range from simple designs to more complex and creative ones—from traditional locker-hooked projects to new and exciting looks, such as extra-long loops. There's plenty here for you if you're looking to go beyond the basics. If you're looking for classic locker-hooked projects, you'll find some of those here, as well. For classic rug designs check out the Striped Mosaic Patio Rug on page 108 or the Spiral Squares Rug on page 118. Often, the best designs for rugs are those that are simple to produce, like these two designs. To achieve beautiful locker-hooked projects, check out my collection of key tips on page 35.

I am always on the hunt to discover new supplies and try new craft products and tools. As a result, I'm constantly coming up with new design ideas and I just can't wait to share a group of them with you in these pages. I recently discovered a pliable netting that led me to explore using extra-long loops in designs. It's perfect for creating wearables and accents. In addition to new materials, I also have new techniques that will help you develop projects that explode with color and texture. This book explores new ways of unveiling these qualities with new materials and ideas for framing, hooking a design and layering on texture.

I love the texture traditional locker hooking techniques can produce, but on occasion some of the beautiful designs in fabrics can be hooked away. So, in order to feature special designs or colors in my looping material, I created a brand new technique I call *ruched frames*. When combined with locker hooking techniques, it can create beautiful, plush shapes that show more of the design and rich colors in fabrics, ribbons and novelty yarn.

Even as I write this I have several projects in the works that aren't going to be finished in time to make it into this book. Stay tuned to my website (colorcrazy.com) to get a sneak peek at new projects as I continue to explore and share new techniques and designs. It is my hope that you'll be inspired to try your hand at creating your own locker-hooked designs.

CHAPTER ONE

Getting Started

In my first book, *Hook, Loop & Lock,* I covered the basic supplies and techniques for locker hooking. In this book, you will see those basics again, plus I will introduce you to some new materials, techniques and ideas. We'll explore creating more texture in a project and highlighting the materials you choose. One way we'll do both of these things is with an exciting new technique I call *ruched frames.* This technique produces padded shapes that will add a whole new dimension to your projects. And, you'll get double the design ideas because you can choose to use these ruched frame elements or you can replace them with additional locker hooking if you desire.

In addition to new techniques, you'll learn about new materials like pliable 6 mesh canvas netting; you can use this canvas to incorporate big loops in wearables and accents. There are also essential tips throughout this chapter that will help you produce beautiful, well-made projects. All you have to do is pick a project (or have a design idea in mind), choose your materials and read on to get started.

Supplies

You only need a few basic supplies and tools to start locker hooking—a base material such as mesh canvas, locking medium, a decorative material for hooking, a locker hook, scissors and a tapestry needle. These supplies and materials can be used not only to produce traditional locker-hooked rugs, but also in creative ways to produce unique designs. And, if you want to go beyond basics, there's a wide variety of materials you can choose from, especially when it comes to decorative hooking materials. Once you start branching out from fabric to materials like ribbon and yarn, you'll start seeing all kinds of craft supplies in a new light, and I'm sure you'll quickly find yourself working all kinds of materials into your locker-hooked projects.

BASE MATERIALS

There are two main materials I recommend as a base for locker-hooked projects: rug canvas and burlap. Use the descriptions below to choose the base that is right for your project.

Rug Canvas

Rug canvas is classified by the number of squares per inch in the mesh. Remember to match your canvas not only to your project, but also to your decorative hooking material—the larger the mesh in the canvas, the wider your hooking material should be. If you're using fabric as hooking material, the weight of your fabric should also influence which canvas you use.

3.3 Mesh Canvas: This canvas has the widest mesh available that I've been able to find. It can be purchased online and in some rug hooking or craft stores. This canvas is ideal for rugs or other items hooked with heavy, thick fabrics.

3.75 Mesh Canvas: This is the most popular locker hooking canvas available and the easiest to find. Most craft stores carry this. It's primarily used for rugs, but you can also use it to make tote bags, trivets, coasters and ornaments.

5 Mesh Canvas: Canvas of this size can be found online and in some craft stores. It's a finer mesh that allows you to create more detailed work in rugs, runners and mats. It's also ideal for smaller projects like jewelry or ornaments.

6 Mesh Canvas Netting: For me, this canvas was an amazing new discovery. It is a pliable, yet sturdy, netting that is ideal for wearables. It may not be sturdy enough for a rug, but it is great for a throw. I use it to create wearable projects such as the Bolero Sweater with Loopy Collar and Cuffs design featured on page 56. It's not yet broadly available, but you can find it online.

Burlap and Linen Burlap

Burlap is a roughly woven fabric made of jute that can be used for locker hooking simple designs. Linen burlap is made from flax instead of jute and is great for detailed rug hooking; it is especially useful when you only want to hook a portion of the base and want the remainder to show, such as in the Dahlia Ring Bearer's Pillow on page 58. You can find linen burlap in a variety of base colors in some fabric stores and online.

LOCKING MEDIUM AND RUCHED FRAME PADDING

These materials support the decorative portions of your projects; because they provide support, they should be sturdy. Locking medium runs through the decorative loops to hold them in place, while ruched frame padding lines your base to elevate the decorative portions of ruched frames.

Cotton Twine: This is the original locking medium for locker-hooked rugs. It is a sturdy solution to locking your loops in place, especially for rugs. White was used traditionally, but for circular projects with vibrant colors, try a sturdy black yarn or cotton twine. Designs like these may have locking medium showing between loops in places where the design bends; using a black locking medium helps hide these spaces.

Matching Yarn: For some projects, especially wearables, a matching yarn can be the best locking medium. This will provide a clean and smooth look in your designs; if the locking medium shows through, it will blend into the decorative loops.

Ruched Frame Padding: Use something that will make for a plush filling, like a medium- to heavy-weight wool or wool blend yarn to create padding for ruched frame designs. Try a few different materials to find one that provides the level of padding you desire.

DECORATIVE HOOKING MATERIAL

Your choices for decorative hooking material are nearly endless—if you can pull up loops of a material, and it creates the effect you desire, you can use it. And don't limit yourself to just one material—multiple materials can be used in combination to create different textures, or you can layer one material on top of another. One of the great things about locker hooking is that you can use up your stash of fabrics and yarns, and you can recycle garments to produce spectacular locker-hooked creations. Whether you use quilting quality cotton fabric, hand-dyed batiks, silks, ribbon, yarn, wool strips, unspun fibers or your own hand-dyed creations, take time to explore combining different materials to create unique effects in your own designs.

Cotton Fabric: Quilting quality cotton fabric is a traditional, and widely available, choice for decorative hooking material. If you like, you can purchase yardage and cut it into strips for locker hooking (see page 15). You can also buy pre-cut strips of printed and hand-dyed fabric online and in some craft and fabric stores.

Other Fabrics: Many other fabrics can be torn or cut into strips and used for decorative hooking material, including denim, muslin, osnaburg, jersey knits, or even synthetics. Wool fabrics, a favorite among traditional rug hookers, are wonderful in locker hooking. They're available in a variety of hand-dyed colors and you can cut your own or buy them already cut. Silk fabric is ideal as an accent or for smaller locker-hooked designs. It's a more expensive option but if you're making something special, silk is a wonderful addition. Sari ribbons are already pre-cut and perfect for locker hooking. When loosely woven silk fabrics are torn, you get wonderful frayed edges. The juxtaposition of a natural non-dyed fabric like osnaburg against silk strips with frayed edges (like you'll see in the Rags and Silk Evening Bag on page 42) is amazing.

Yarn: There is a never-ending variety of yarn to choose from and use in locker hooking. Yarns in heavier weights can be used alone, while thin yarns can be layered on top of fabric strips to create a more textured feel. Try yarn in rugs, pillows and wearables. While it is not technically yarn, jute twine can be used layered with fabric just like yarn. It is available in a variety of colors, but I like using this in its natural color to frame rugs, mats, coasters and table runners.

Ribbon: Ribbon can be used in a variety of ways for your projects; it is a great accent in locker hooking, or can be used as an embellishment. Try tying pieces of ribbon around the edge of a project for fringe. One of my favorite kinds of ribbon for locker hooking is hand-dyed silk ribbon—it's available in rich, variegated color combinations. I also like to use seam binding ribbon, which, as its name suggests, is traditionally used to bind seams. This type of ribbon is available in a wide assortment of colors and is great for framing edges and accenting locker-hooked designs.

Unspun Fiber: I love locker hooking with unspun fiber. It can be more difficult to locker hook than fabric, yarn or ribbon, and will require patience, but the results are incredible. Unspun mohair locks are especially beautiful as accents—see the Ho, Ho, Ho! Santa Ornament on page 76.

Recycled Materials: You can repurpose apparel and other materials to use in locker hooking. Try cutting up old jeans, T-shirts, woven cotton shirts, jersey knits, or even plastic bags to create strips for locker hooking.

GET CREATIVE AND EMBELLISH!

You can embellish your designs with glitter, buttons, felt, silk flowers, ribbons, beads, charms, paint, and much more. You can make your own accents by painting wood or metal elements. My latest craze is vintage buttons and metal filigree pieces. While pretty much anything goes with embellishments, sometimes a little goes a long way. Choose what works for you and have fun adding extra sparkle to your designs! Learn more about adding embellishments to your projects on page 34.

TOOLS

There are only a few tools you need to start locker hooking, but there are a few more beyond the basics that you might find helpful. I've included information about all of them here, along with my own preferences. If possible, before you buy, try tools in a variety of styles and brands and choose the one that is easiest and most comfortable for you to use.

Locker Hook: This is your main tool for locker hooking; it has a hook at one end for pulling up loops and a needle eye at the other end for carrying locking medium. Locker hooks are widely available in both aluminum and steel, and some handcrafted locker hooks are available in wood and other materials. I prefer an aluminum locker hook because it feels lighter and easier to use in my hand. Try out different locker hooks to see which is easiest for you to use and stick with whatever feels best.

Yarn or Tapestry Needle: You'll need a large needle for framing and assembling locker-hooked pieces. I like using a #13 tapestry needle for finishing locker-hooked projects. A slightly larger or smaller needle will work as well.

Sewing Needle: I also recommend keeping traditional sewing needles (also called "sharps") for stitching embellishments or a lining to your project. Use whatever weight sewing needle will work best with your materials.

Heavy-Duty Scissors or Shears: Choose a pair of heavy-duty scissors for tough cutting jobs, like cutting rug canvas.

Fine Craft or Sewing Scissors: A small pair of fine, sharp scissors is essential for cutting fabric and ribbon.

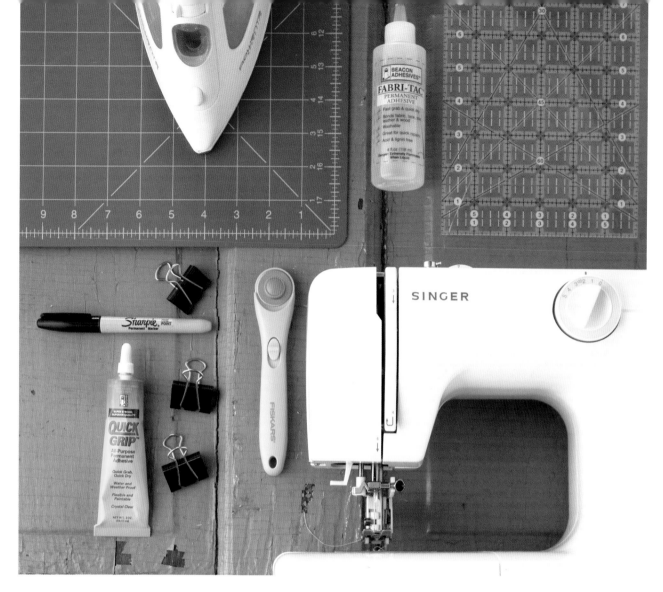

Ruler: Always handy for just about any craft, for locker hooking you'll use a ruler for measuring and cutting fabric.

Rotary Cutter and Self-Healing Mat: A rotary cutter is a tool used by quilters for quickly cutting fabric. While I prefer tearing my cotton fabric strips, you can also cut your strips, and a rotary cutter is faster and easier to use than scissors. Also, for some fabrics that don't tear easily, like knit fabrics, it's easiest to use a rotary cutter. If you're using a rotary cutter, you'll also need a self-healing mat; it will protect your tabletop when you are cutting fabric with a rotary cutter (and prevent your rotary cutter blade from going dull).

Fast Drying Adhesive: I often use a small bead of glue to secure knots on items that need additional support, and glue can also come in handy when you want to attach embellishments or a lining. There are a lot of adhesive products on the market, but I prefer using Beacon's Fabri-Tac or Quick Grip. They're permanent,

dry fast and work on fabric, canvas and various other materials. Fabri-Tac is the thinner of the two and works well on fabric, felt and lighter embellishments. You can use it to attach linings easily instead of stitching. Quick Grip is gel-like and works on fabric but is great for use with ceramics, glass, metal, beads and various other heavier embellishments. It can also be used to attach a heavier or thicker lining.

Sewing Machine: You can use a sewing machine to secure the edges of your canvas for larger projects like a rug, or when sewing linings.

Iron: A standard steam iron is handy to keep on hand for steam pressing fabric, including regular burlap and linen burlap base material.

Permanent Markers: You can use permanent markers for tracing patterns on your canvas. Keep multiple colors on hand for marking complex patterns.

Clamps or Binder Clips: Keep a few of these available to hold projects together while glue dries.

Techniques

Whether you're new to locker hooking, or a practiced hand at it, there are techniques and tips for you over the following pages. If you're starting from scratch, begin with Preparing Fabric for Locker Hooking below and proceed from there. If you're looking to take your locker hooking in new directions, check out Ruched Frames on page 28.

PREPARING FABRIC FOR LOCKER HOOKING

A bit of care for your fabric in the beginning will make the process of locker hooking more pleasant and your finished project look its best.

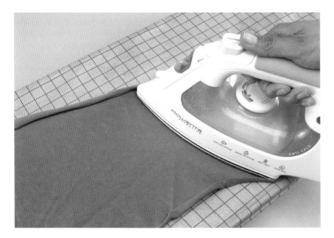

Wash, Dry and Press

Most store-bought fabrics are pre-shrunk, so it is not necessary to wash them if you don't wish to. However, if you're using a fabric that may shrink, or if you're hooking a project you'll want to wash, wash and dry the fabric before using it. Also, if you've hand-dyed your fabrics, wash and dry the fabric so that there is no excess dye in the fabric. If the fabric you are using has selvages, cut them off. Use a steam iron to press any fabric that is wrinkled before you cut or tear it.

Options for Creating Strips

After you've chosen your locker hooking material and washed, dried and pressed it as needed, it's time to create strips for locker hooking. The width of the strips depends on the weight of the fabric and the canvas base you are using—see the chart below for approximate measurements and find additional information on page 35.

Creating Strips with a Rotary Cutter

While using a rotary cutter is not my preferred method for creating strips, it is very popular and has its benefits. For instance, if you use a rotary cutter your strips will have clean edges; you can also use a rotary cutter to cut some fabrics that do not tear well. Begin by cutting the edge of the fabric so it is straight. Use a ruler to guide your rotary cutter as you cut the strips.

	LIGHT-WEIGHT FABRICS (SUCH AS SILK)	MEDIUM-WEIGHT FABRICS (SUCH AS QUILTING COTTON)	HEAVY-WEIGHT FABRICS (SUCH AS DENIM)
3.3 MESH	$1\frac{1}{2}$"–$2\frac{1}{4}$" (4cm–5.5cm)	1"–$1\frac{3}{4}$" (2.5cm–4.5cm)	$\frac{1}{2}$"–1" (1.5cm–2.5cm)
3.75 MESH	$1\frac{1}{2}$"–2" (4cm–5cm)	$\frac{3}{4}$"–1" (2cm–2.5cm)	$\frac{1}{2}$"–$\frac{3}{4}$" (1.5cm–2cm)
5 MESH	$\frac{3}{4}$"–1" (2cm–2.5cm)	$\frac{1}{2}$"–$\frac{3}{4}$" (1.5cm–2cm)	$\frac{1}{4}$" (6mm)
6 MESH	$\frac{1}{4}$"–$\frac{1}{2}$" (6mm–1.5cm)	$\frac{1}{4}$"–$\frac{1}{2}$" (6mm–1.5cm)	do not combine

Creating Strips by Tearing

While tearing doesn't work on all fabrics, I prefer tearing woven cotton fabric because it goes much faster than cutting. Don't be concerned about cotton fraying as you tear—when you locker hook strips, you fold the edges under and any fraying is hidden as you pull up loops. For some projects, you may prefer the frayed edges for added texture.

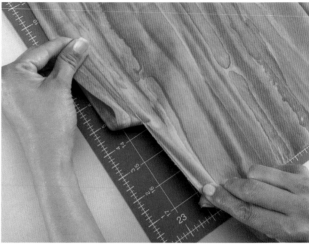

1 Notch the edge of your fabric with scissors or a rotary cutter. Space each notch a strip's width apart (see the chart on page 15 for strip width).

2 Grasp the fabric with one hand on each side of a notch. Tear a strip of fabric off of the yardage.

DON'T BE AFRAID TO FRAY

You can create wonderful texture by tearing some fabrics. Loosely woven silks and some cotton fabrics like denim and osnaburg will fray beautifully when torn or cut. Take advantage of this! Pull off extra strings on the edges to create more fraying for added texture. Check out the Rags and Silk Evening Bag on page 42 or the Spiral Squares Rug on page 118 to see frayed fabrics in action.

MEASUREMENTS FROM YARDAGE INTO STRIPS

The materials lists for the projects in this book measure the amount of decorative looping material you'll need in yards (meters). This chart shows you how many yards (meters) of strips you'll get from a yard (meter) of fabric so you can easily calculate how much fabric to buy for a project.

1 yd. (.9m) of fabric (44" × 36" [112cm × 91.5cm]) cut into ½" (1.5cm) strips = 88 yds. (80.5m) of fabric strips

1 yd. (.9m) of fabric (44" × 36" [112cm × 91.5cm]) cut into ¾" (2cm) strips = 58 yds. (53m) of fabric strips

1 yd. (.9m) of fabric (44" × 36" [112cm × 91.5cm]) cut into 1" (2.5cm) strips = 44 yds. (40.2m) of fabric strips

PREPARING A BASE FOR LOCKER HOOKING

Once your fabric is ready, it's time to prepare a base for your project. This process is simple, but it plays a very important role in both the appearance and quality of your finished project. Follow these steps for a project that looks great and lasts!

Preparing a Square or Rectangular Base

If your project is a square or rectangle, such as the Summer Garden Vine Runner on page 94, the steps below will help you get ready to start locker hooking.

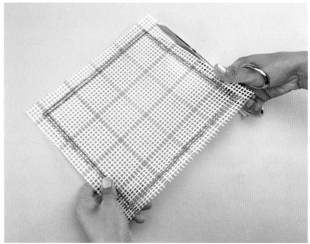

1 Using the dimensions listed in the project's instructions, mark the outline of the finished piece on the canvas.

2 Double check that the area marked is the correct size. Missing just one square can throw off your entire project. Once you're sure your outline is in the right place, cut the canvas, leaving excess squares around the edge for folding under—the instructions for your project will let you know exactly how many squares to fold under.

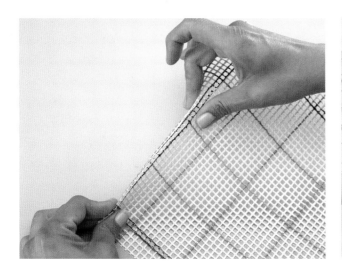

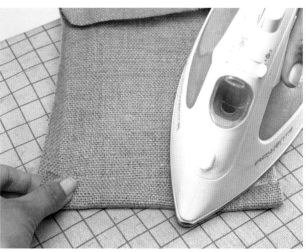

3 Fold over the excess canvas around the edges of the piece of base material and secure the fold by creasing the canvas with your hands.

4 For a mesh canvas base, creasing the canvas with your hands will be enough for the edge to stay under. If it is not for some reason, or if you are using burlap as your base, iron the fold.

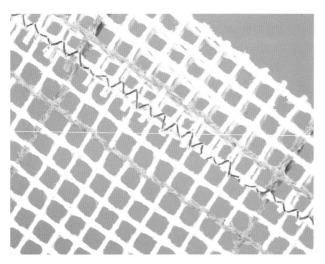

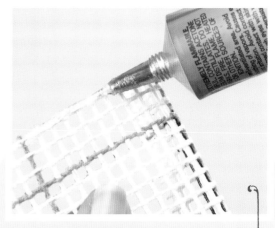

5 If you are making a large piece, or a piece that will need to stand up to a lot of wear and tear, like a rug, after you fold over the edge, use a sewing machine to secure the folded edges. Zig zag stitch using tapestry thread. This will allow you to wash your project in the gentle cycle of a washing machine.

SECURING SMALL PIECES

If your project requires a small amount of canvas that will remain unfolded or will overlap when working in the round, secure the edges with permanent glue before locker hooking. This prevents the canvas from unraveling.

Preparing a Shaped Base

Special shapes require special care—and each base has its own special steps. Following these instructions will help you prepare a base for a shaped project, such as the Oh, Christmas Tree! Ornament on page 74.

Mesh Canvas Shaped Base

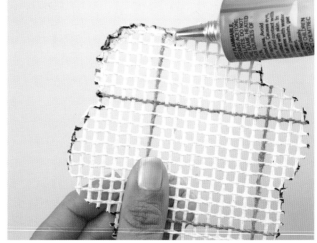

1 If your shaped project will be created on mesh rug canvas, lay the canvas over your template and trace the pattern onto the canvas. If your project is on burlap or linen burlap, see page 19.

2 Cut the canvas directly along the traced line, then apply a line of glue around the canvas piece to completely cover all edges. Allow the glue to dry completely before locker hooking. The glue will keep the canvas from unraveling.

Burlap Shaped Base

 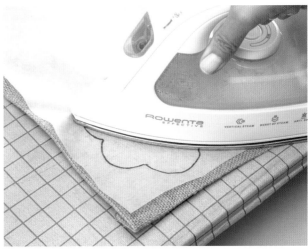

1 I recently learned of iron-on transfer pens—this was a great find, especially for transferring designs onto burlap and linen burlap. To begin, lay a piece of tracing paper over your design. Use the iron-on transfer pen to trace your design onto the tracing paper.

2 Follow the manufacturer's instructions to transfer the design from the tracing paper to the burlap or linen burlap.

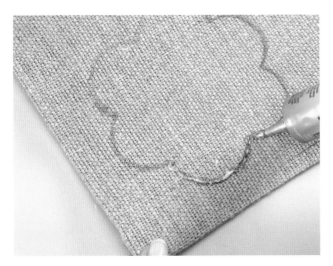 

3 Apply a substantial line of glue along the pattern edge. Let the glue dry completely.

4 Cut out the design just outside the glue line.

LAYERS OF COLOR

You can start adding color to your project right at the base. If the base of your project will show anywhere in the project, you can add to its appearance by painting it. Acrylic paints, fabric paints and spray paint work well. I especially like using metallic paints for extra sparkle, like luminescent Lumiere paints from Jacquard Products. For many paints, at least two coats will be needed for full coverage. Let the paint on the canvas or burlap dry completely before you begin locker hooking.

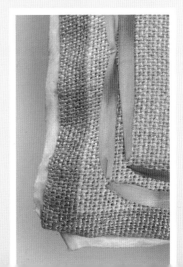

Framing the Base

For rugs and other stand-alone projects that don't require assembly, like the Spring Stripes Placemat on page 98, start by framing the edge of your canvas. This will not only provide protection to the edge of the piece, making it sturdier and longer lasting, but it will also add to the look of the project, especially if you choose one of the more decorative options on page 21. For projects that will be assembled from multiple locker-hooked pieces, you will locker hook each piece first, assemble, and then frame the assembled project.

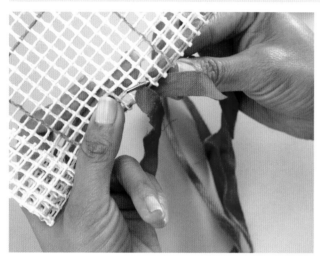

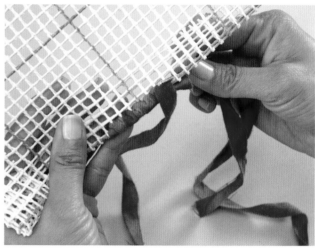

1 Thread a 1½ yd.–2 yd. (1.4m–1.8m) strip of decorative hooking material through your locker hook or a tapestry needle. (I find it easiest to use a tapestry needle for framing.) Follow the project instructions to determine the width of the strip.

Pull the fabric strip through a square directly at the edge of the canvas from front to back, leaving a 2" (5cm) tail. To take the next stitch, bring the needle through the next square in the canvas from back to front.

2 Continue to whipstitch along the edge of the canvas, taking each stitch from back to front and making sure each stitch lays flat along the edge of the canvas. Stitch around the tail of the fabric strip to conceal and secure it.

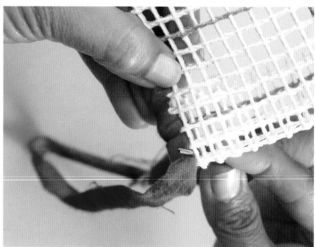

3 When you reach the last stitch on the edge, take a stitch into the square from back to front.

4 To cover the corner, turn the canvas 90 degrees and stitch into the same stitch again. You may need to add a third stitch to the same square to completely cover the corner. Continue working around the project until every part of the outer edge is covered.

FRAMING BURLAP

Framing burlap can be a little trickier than framing mesh canvas; without squares to follow, you'll need to take care that your stitches are even and equally spaced. Use the same whipstitch technique to wrap the edge of the burlap or linen burlap using a tapestry needle with ribbon or yarn (double up yarn as needed for complete coverage).

DECORATIVE FRAMING

On page 24 we'll discuss how to add more texture and color to a project by locker hooking with more than one material. You can use this trick in your frame, as well. For instance, you can add jute twine or contrasting ribbon or yarn to a fabric frame. To do this, just whipstitch over the finished fabric frame with a contrasting material. This additional accent can add a beautiful layered look.

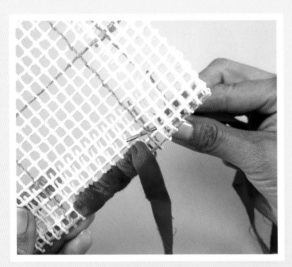

One easy way to give your project's frame more visual punch is to widen it. You can see in the picture above how a wider frame compares to a standard frame.

To make a wide frame, use the steps outlined on page 20, but instead of whipstitching into the row of squares at the edge of the canvas, make your stitches in the second row of squares from the edge. For a wider, more dramatic frame you could even stitch further into the canvas. A wide frame works well for rugs, runners and ornaments.

LOCKER HOOKING BASICS

Now you're ready to start locker hooking! Locker hooking consists of pulling up loops through a base material, then using locking medium to secure the loops in place. There are different ways to locker hook, although these basic actions are the same for each method—flip to page 26 to check the methods out! The instructions for each project in this book will let you know what method, or methods, to use.

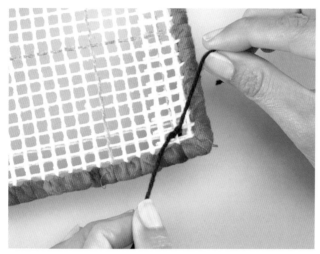

1 Thread a 2 yd. (1.8m) length of locking medium (or whatever length you're comfortable with) through the eye of your locker hook. If you like, you can tie your locking medium to the base. This isn't essential, but it will stop you from pulling your locking medium completely through and out of your decorative loops.

2 Thread the eye of the locker hook with locking medium. Push the hook end of the locker hook through the base material from front to back. Catch the decorative looping material (here, a strip of cotton fabric) with your hook.

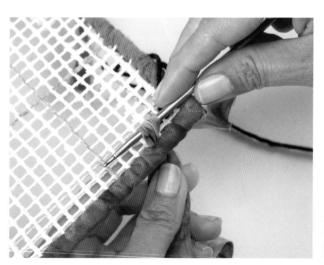

3 Pull a loop of your decorative material up through the base to the front. The loop should be a minimum of ¼" (6mm) in height. If your loop is smaller than this, it can be difficult to pull the locker hook through the loops later.

4 Push the locker hook through the next square in the canvas and pull up another loop. Give it a tug to match the height of the first loop. Continue pulling up loops until you have 4-6 on your locker hook (you can pull up as few or as many as you wish, but I've found that this is a good range for beginners). Remember to give each loop a tug to match the height of the other loops on the hook.

5 Pull the locker hook through the loops you've pulled up. Pull the locking medium into the loops to secure them in place.

LONGER LOOPS

Try varying the loop length in your projects—pulling up long loops allows you to create a fun accent or an essential look in a design. You can pull up medium loops ($1/2$"–1" [1.5cm–2.5cm]) and use locking medium to hold them in place just as you would shorter loops. For extra-long loops ($1^1/2$" [4cm] and longer) like those shown in the Loopy Collar design on page 56, the locking medium will be more visible and may not stay in place. Use the techniques shown on page 32 to secure extra long loops.

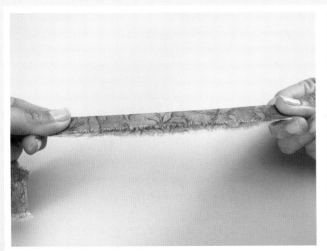

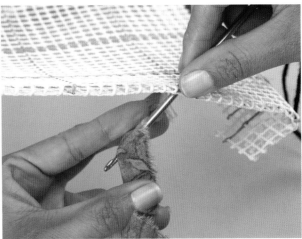

USING PRINTED FABRICS

If you choose to use a printed fabric—or any fabric with a right and a wrong side—for locker hooking, use this method to keep the wrong side of the fabric from showing: Cut the strips wider than you would for reversible fabrics (see the chart on page 15). When you are ready to begin locker hooking, fold the fabric strip in half and pull up folded loops to hide the unprinted side.

BEYOND THE BASICS

Once you have the most basic steps of locker hooking down—pulling up loops and locking them in place—it's time to add more skills to your locker hooking repertoire. Over these pages you'll learn several techniques, including the different locker hooking methods and ways to add more visual interest to your projects.

Attaching Additional Decorative Hooking Material

If you are locker hooking anything other than a very small project, you're bound to come to the end of your decorative hooking material sooner or later. When this happens, you can merely drop your strip and start with a new one, but this will leave you with lots of tails to sew in. Use the method below to attach new strips and you'll greatly reduce the time it takes to neatly finish a project. (This method truly comes in handy when you're using small swatches of fabric for locker hooking!) This technique works best on quilting-weight cotton fabrics and other fabrics of similiar weight. Do not join the strips of heavy-weight fabrics in this manner.

 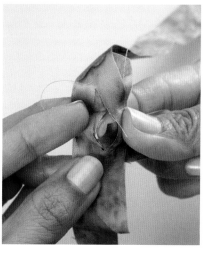 

1 Cut the end of the strip you've been working with and the new strip on a diagonal. Layer the strips, fold them approximately 3/4" (2cm) from the end and cut a 1/2" (1.5cm) slit in the center of the strips.

2 Unfold the strips and push the tail of the new strip through the slit in both strips.

3 Gently pull on both strips until they snug up to each other at the slit. This process can be tricky at first, so keep practicing until the strips line up neatly.

Locker Hooking with Multiple Materials

If you want to add more color and texture to a project, you can pull up loops with different strips of material held together. Try fabric with ribbon, yarn or twine. Mohair yarn can add a soft fuzziness to a project—see the Meadowlands Fibers Purse on page 72 for an example. Fabric and twine together can add a homespun touch to a project; I used this combination in the Spring Stripes Placemat on page 98. Locker hooking mixed elements can add layers of texture and color to create a more sophisticated look.

Switching Strips

Whether you're switching strips to change colors, to change materials or because you've reached the end of a strip and need to start a new one, this quick and easy process will get you started on a new strip.

1 If you are switching strips because you've reached the end of a strip, stop locker hooking when there is a 1½"–2" (4cm–5cm) tail left. If you are switching to a new color or material, you can merely drop the strip you are working with when you are ready to switch strips.

Pick up the new strip, leaving a 1½"–2" (4cm–5cm) tail, and bring it to the back of the base. Hook the new strip with the locker hook.

2 Pull up a loop with the new strip in the square next to where you stopped working with the strip you dropped. Continue locker hooking with the new strip, following your pattern.

Traveling Strips

When you're working on a design that involves using the same color in different places, you can travel the fabric strip across the back of the piece from one area to another. Traveling keeps you from starting and stopping strips repeatedly and creating extra tails that will need to be sewn in later. When you have reached the point in your design where you are ready to switch back to a color or material you have previously used, examine

the back of your piece. You can travel a strip from one area to another as long as the space between the two areas has already been locker hooked. In the project shown here I started a row of loops with blue fabric, I switched to green fabric, and now later in the same row I'm switching back to blue. I'll be traveling the blue strip behind the area hooked in green. Do not travel strips over unhooked areas—if you do, it will be difficult to hook in those areas later! Once you've determined that you can travel from one point to another, pull the fabric strip you wish to travel across the back of the piece from its current location to the new area. Make sure the strip lays flat against the back of the piece. Continue locker hooking, following your pattern.

METHODS OF LOCKER HOOKING

The goal of locker hooking is to fill a design with hooked loops of material. You can use different methods to accomplish this. Each method gives a project its own distinct look, so be sure to take advantage of each method's qualities. You can also combine methods, like I did in the Summer Poppy Mat on page 120.

Linear Locker Hooking

This method is the easiest, and it is the one I suggest for your first projects. The look this method gives to a project works best with geometric patterns, especially stripes.

1 Starting at one side of the canvas, pull up loops straight across a single row of canvas, switching materials or colors as required by your pattern.

2 When you reach the end of the row you're working, turn the canvas 180 degrees and work the next row in the opposite direction, again changing colors or materials as your pattern demands. Continue working one row at a time until you complete the project.
  To create the neatest look when locker hooking in the linear method, work one spiral row inside the frame as I have here before you begin linear locker hooking. This covers the ends of the rows where you change direction, which can leave the locking medium exposed.

Spiral Locker Hooking

The spiral method is an easy one as well, but it gives the finished project a slightly different appearance because the direction of the hooking is constantly changing. This method is best when your design has concentric elements.

1 You can work in a spiral either from the center of a piece outward, or from the outer edge inward. To work from the outside in, start at one corner of the canvas and pull up loops across a single row of canvas, switching colors or materials as required by your pattern.

2 When you reach the end of the row you're working, turn the canvas 90 degrees and work the next row perpendicular to the first, again changing colors as your pattern demands. Continue working in a concentric spiral until you complete the project.

Free Form Locker Hooking

Free form locker hooking is a more difficult technique, but it is perfect for detailed designs. You can use this technique on all canvas types but it shows details best on 5 mesh canvas. Using this method you can create various elements, outline them, and then fill them in, allowing more vivid and detailed projects with a great sense of movement.

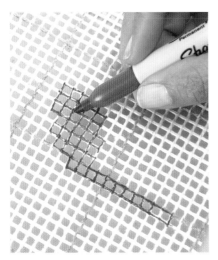

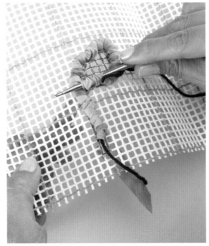

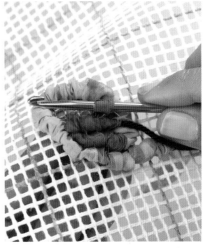

1 Mark the pattern you'll be following on your canvas with permanent markers. You can do this for any method, but it's especially helpful for free form locker hooking.

2 Start locker hooking following your design. Choose one element to start with; if the element has multiple parts, like the one above, start hooking the outer element first.

3 Work inward to fill in the design, switching colors as instructed by your pattern. Continue locker hooking until the entire element is complete. Move on to the next element and repeat.

Locker Hooking in the Round

When locker hooking circular projects like baskets, your project will be sturdiest if you work in the round, rather than working flat and assembling the project to form a circle later. Follow these easy steps to transform your canvas from flat to round.

1 Prepare your canvas and treat the edges as directed by your pattern. Begin pulling up loops several inches from one edge of the canvas. Work toward the edge. When you are 4-5 squares from the edge, overlap the ends of the canvas and bring the locker hook through both pieces of canvas.

2 Continue to locker hook following your pattern, working through both thicknesses of canvas where they overlap.

3 If your pattern calls for the canvas to be framed, do so according to the pattern instructions.

A NEW TECHNIQUE: RUCHED FRAMES

This is a great technique that adds a new texture to your locker-hooked projects. As I mentioned previously, this technique really shows off the decorative materials you use because they show over more extended areas, rather than small loops. It isn't difficult to do, it looks beautiful, and it can fill in spaces very quickly in a design. To practice ruched frames, try the Vineyard Leaves Belt design featured on page 44; it is basically one long ruched frame with a clasp added.

Straight Ruched Frames

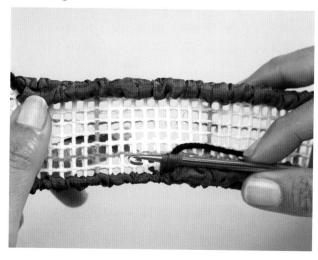

1 Before you begin the ruched frame, frame your canvas and outline the ruched portion of the design with a row of locker hooking.

2 Thread a tapestry needle with your ruched frame padding material (I recommend a medium- to heavy-weight wool or wool blend yarn). Start stitching at one end of the design to fill in the ruched frame area, taking small stitches on the backside and long stitches (covering at least 8–12 squares) on the front.

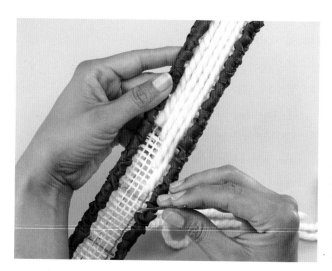

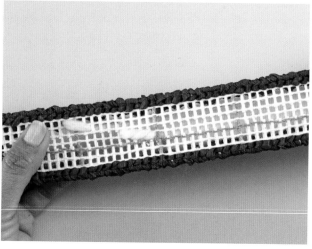

3 Stitch until the area is filled. For extra-long spaces, like belts or handles, stagger your long stitches by altering their length on a diagonal line. If you were to line up your stitches and not stagger them, there would be a break in the padding that could show under the ruched frame.

4 As you work, check the back of your piece to make sure that you are only taking small stitches from one area to the next on the back of the piece so that the back is not padded like the front.

5 Thread a tapestry needle with a ½"–1½" (1.5cm–4cm) wide fabric or ribbon strip. Leave a 1½" (4cm) tail and begin stitching over the canvas and padding. Start along the same row where the frame is locker hooked and wrap the strip around the frame area perpendicular to the padding. Take care to not wrap too tightly and make sure you cover the entire padded area so that none of the padding shows through.

6 As you stitch, check the back of the project as well to make sure you are getting full coverage. Fluff the strips on the front or back and arrange by hand if necessary to completely cover the canvas and padding.

Shaped Ruched Frames

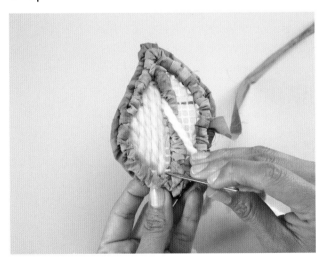

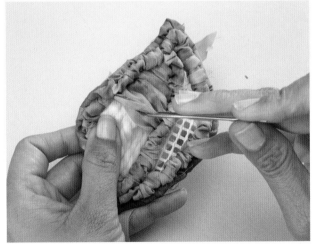

1 Begin as for a straight ruched frame by framing your canvas and locker hooking the outline of the ruched frame area. Begin filling in the ruched frame area with ruched frame padding material, filling the available space. Again, make long fill stitches on the front but take small stitches on the back so that only the front is padded.

2 Thread a tapestry needle with a ½"–1½" (1.5cm–4cm) wide fabric or ribbon strip. Leave a 1½" (4cm) tail and begin stitching over the canvas and padding. Start at one end of the ruched frame area and work toward the other, wrapping the strip around the frame area perpendicular to the padding. Don't wrap too tightly and make sure you cover the entire padded area.

FINISHING TECHNIQUES

When your locker hooking is finished, your project isn't. There are a few more steps to go so that your project will look its best and last a long time. If you take care with these last few steps, you'll be rewarded with a project you can be proud of!

Sewing in Tails

The first finishing step toward a polished look for your project is to sew in the tails of decorative hooking material and locking medium. Securing these ends keeps a project looking tidy and helps keep everything in its place.

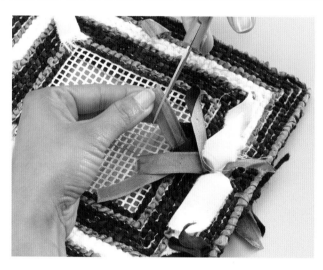

1 Trim all of the decorative hooking material tails to approximately 2" (5cm). Trim the tails on the diagonal to make it easy to thread them through the eye of your locker hook.

2 Push the eye end of your locker hook through the project from front to back through a square close to a tail of decorative hooking material. Thread the tail through the eye of the locker hook.

3 Pull the tail of decorative hooking material to the front of the piece. Starting approximately five squares away from the tail, thread the eye end of the locker hook through decorative loops, working back toward the tail of hooking material.

4 Thread the tail through the eye of the locker hook again.

5 Use the locker hook to pull the tail through the loops the locker hook was threaded through. Wriggle the hook to help pull the tail through.

6 Trim off the tail close to the surface of the project near the last loop.

7 For tails of locking medium, begin by repeating Steps 3-4; thread the eye of the locker hook through decorative loops toward the tail of locking medium. Thread the locking medium tail through the eye of the locker hook.

8 Pull the locking medium tail through the decorative loops and trim the rest of the tail off close to the surface of the project near the last loop.

Adding a Lining

Another step you can take to give your project a nicely finished look is to add a lining. A lining covers all the lumps, bumps and knots on the back of a piece and also helps protect the piece and makes it sturdier. There are a few ways you can line a project.

Sewn Lining

A sewn lining is the best choice for projects that will be washed or for projects where the back will show. To create a sewn lining, cut and press your lining fabric, then fold over a seam allowance on each edge and press it under. Hand stitch the lining to the project with small stitches to provide a nicely finished backing.

Self-Adhesive Fabric Lining

This is the quickest and easiest lining method, but it is also the least secure. The adhesive on self-adhesive fabric is not washable, and is not extremely strong. Use this method for pieces that will not be washed and that will be treated gently.

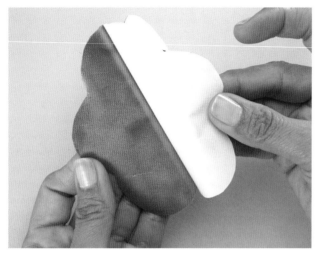

1 Cut the self-adhesive fabric to the size or shape indicated by your pattern. Remove the backing from the fabric.

2 Align the adhesive side of the fabric with your project carefully, then press the fabric onto the project to secure it.

Glued Lining and Securing Long Loops

This method does not produce a look that is as neat and finished as a sewn lining, but it is quicker and very secure. This method is excellent for a project that uses extra-long loops because the glue secures the loops very firmly to the base material.

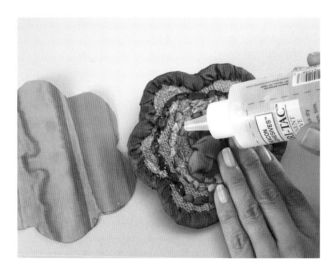

1 Press and cut the fabric for your lining. Generously apply permanent fabric adhesive over the back of the project, especially over areas where decorative hooking material appears.

2 Press the lining fabric into place, carefully aligning the lining with the project. For large projects, use binder clips or clamps to hold the lining in place if necessary. Let the glue dry completely.

Assembling Projects

With locker hooking, assembly has been traditionally used for stitching locker-hooked squares together to form a rug. You can also use this technique to put together pieces for tote bags, boxes, baskets and much more.

1 Align the two locker-hooked pieces following your pattern. Thread a strip of fabric, ribbon or other smooth decorative material through a tapestry needle. Take a stitch through the very edge of the base of both pieces.

2 Continue stitching the two pieces together, taking each stitch in the same direction so the decorative material is whipped around the edges.

3 Ensure that the edge is neatly covered as you stitch, adding additional stitches where needed to cover the edge completely.

4 Once stitching is complete, tie the stitching material in a knot, leaving tails. For added security, add a drop of permanent adhesive to the knot. Sew in the tails to hide them.

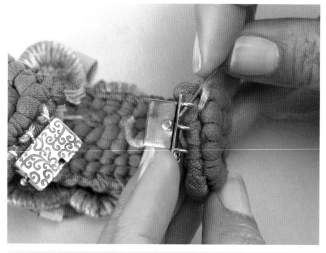

Embellishing Projects

There are nearly endless options for embellishing projects. Try buttons, beads, felted pieces, or anything you find adds the right touch. When it comes to adding embellishments, there are two main ways to secure them: You can either sew embellishments on or use a permanent adhesive to glue them to your project. I recommend sewing for items that will rest on top of the locker hooking, like buttons, beads and charms. For findings like clasps for bracelets or belts, sewing is also my recommendation. For things that would be difficult (or impossible) to secure with sewing, glue will give you a secure hold. I use glue to attach tiles to trivets and pinbacks to brooches, among other uses.

Essential Locker Hooking Tips

❖ **Proper Strip Width:** Use strips of decorative hooking material that have a consistent width and are the correct width for your chosen canvas. If you use strips that are too wide, your design will become bulky and warped. If the strips are too narrow, your locking medium and the canvas will show through. Proper strip width also depends on the weight of the strip material. It's important to test the width of a strip on your chosen mesh canvas before cutting all of the strips. Try locker hooking swatches with strips in different widths to ensure good coverage.

❖ **Consistent Loop Height:** When pulling up loops of fabric, make sure they are at least ¼" (6mm) tall. If your loops are shorter than this, your locking medium will show through and sewing in tails to finish your project will be difficult. Make your loop height consistent, as well. Each time you pull up a loop, give it a tug to match each previous loop. This will help provide a nicely finished look.

❖ **Full, Lofty Loops:** Select heavier locking medium or even double your locking medium to fill and secure decorative loops. This will provide a loftier look for designs, especially rugs. If you use a doubled locking medium, you can make things easier when sewing in tails by clipping the first tail where it hangs, and sewing in the second tail.

❖ **Navigating Tight Corners:** Instead of pulling up several loops at the same time, locker hook tight corners one square at a time to make it easier—especially when using heavy fabric strips.

❖ **Finishing Small Projects:** On smaller projects or projects hooked on linen burlap it's often easier to use a tapestry needle to sew in tails instead of a locker hook.

❖ **Finishing Sharp Corners:** Rounded corners or shapes are easier to frame than sharp corners. To finish sharp corners and get proper coverage with your framing material, add drops of glue to the corner, then whipstitch around the corner, taking care to position the strip to fully cover the corner before the glue dries.

❖ **Care Instructions:** If you intend to machine wash a rug, I recommend using the gentle cycle on the washing machine and drip drying instead of machine drying.

CHAPTER TWO

Gifts and Wearables

For me, there's nothing like presenting someone with a handmade gift. Locker-hooked designs make great gifts that can range from a simple ornament that decorates a gift package to a basket that holds a jar of your own homemade preserves. You can re-create the projects featured in this chapter to make your own gifts, or you can use them as inspiration and then customize them by choosing your own colors and embellishments. I've included a diverse collection of locker-hooked designs from quick and easy projects that can be made in an hour or two, to more complex designs that will take a few afternoons or evenings. And while each of these projects is great for gifting, you can also make yourself a gift or two!

All of the designs in this chapter feature locker hooking, and I also apply the new ruched frame technique to some of these designs. This technique makes for a great purse handle like you'll see in the Meadowlands Fibers Purse on page 72, or an incredible belt—check out the Vineyard Leaves Belt featured on page 44. If you're considering making some locker-hooked Floral Accents based off of the design on page 52, pull out all of your collected beads, ribbons, vintage buttons and other items you can use as accents. It helps to have them at hand for inspiration. If you're like me, I think that once you get started with locker hooking, you may not want to stop!

Garden Preserves Basket

This design came about specifically to carry a jar of preserves as a gift. The idea was to create a pretty basket that would hold a pint canning jar that had vintage appeal. The choice of fabric ended up being an ivory and gold color print and cotton muslin—a perfectly neutral palette that provides a great backdrop for the ivory flower accent. You can recreate this design with similar fabrics or in your favorite combination of colors. You can embellish it like I have with a flower or just tie a bow with a ribbon or set of ribbons. For an added country vintage touch, tie on a gift tag with a length of natural twine. This makes a perfect hostess gift, or a great holiday gift.

TECHNIQUES FOR THIS PROJECT

Preparing a Square or Rectangular Base

Locker Hooking in the Round

Spiral Locker Hooking

Linear Locker Hooking

Sewing in Tails

Assembling Projects

Framing the Base

Embellishing Projects

MATERIALS LIST

5 mesh canvas

10 yds. (9.1m) of ½" (1.5cm) ivory cotton fabric strips

20 yds. (18.3m) of ½" (1.5cm) light yellow printed cotton fabric strips

30 yds. (27.4m) of ½" (1.5cm) beige cotton fabric strips

9 yds. (8.2m) of ½" (1.5cm) amber rayon seam binding

Locking medium (I recommend a sturdy yarn or cotton twine that matches the fabric strips)

Silk flower or embellishment of your choice that matches the fabric strips

Locker hook

Tapestry needle

Scissors

Permanent adhesive

1 Cut three pieces of 5 mesh canvas: a piece 60 squares wide and 36 squares tall for the body of the basket, a piece 21 squares wide and 21 squares tall for the bottom of the basket and a piece 78 squares wide and 10 squares tall for the basket handle. Fold over the edges of each piece of canvas by creasing the row indicated by the gray area in the patterns on page 40 (see Preparing a Square or Rectangular Base on pages 17–18).

2 To make the basket body you will be working in the round (see Locker Hooking in the Round on page 27). Overlap four squares of canvas to make the canvas piece circular and locker hook the basket body following the pattern on page 40.

3 Locker hook the bottom of the basket by following the pattern on page 40 and using the spiral technique (see Spiral Locker Hooking on page 26).

4 Locker hook the basket's handle using the linear method (see Linear Locker Hooking on page 26). Leave five rows of canvas unhooked at each end of the handle.

5 Sew in the fabric and locking medium tails on each piece of the basket (see Sewing in Tails on pages 30–31). Whipstitch the basket body to the bottom of the basket (see Assembling Projects on page 33).

6 Frame the top edge of the basket body and the long edges of the handle with rayon seam binding (see Framing the Base on pages 20–21). Stitch the handle to the basket body with a tapestry needle and rayon seam binding.

7 Sew in any remaining tails. Attach the silk flower or embellishment of your choice with permanent glue (see Embellishing Projects on page 34).

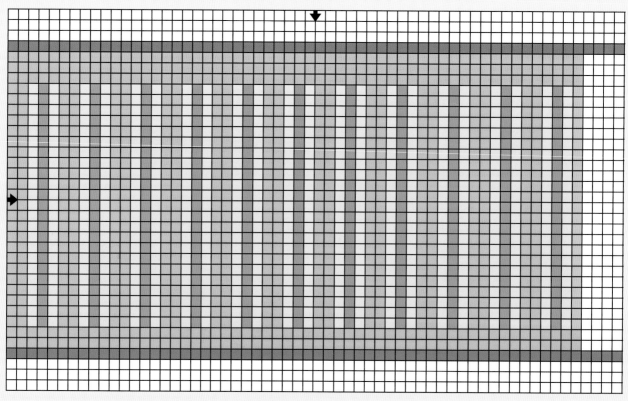

Garden Preserves Basket (body)

(project instructions appear on page 39)

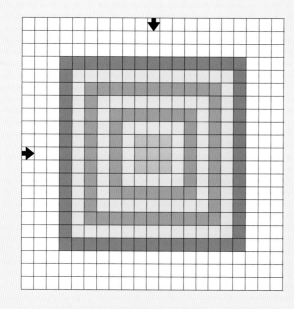

Garden Preserves Basket (bottom)

(project instructions appear on page 39)

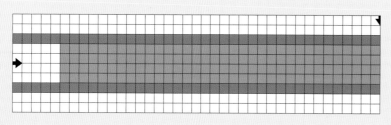

Garden Preserves Basket (handle)

(project instructions appear on page 39)

This chart shows half of the handle. To complete the handle, work from left to right, then repeat the chart from right to left.

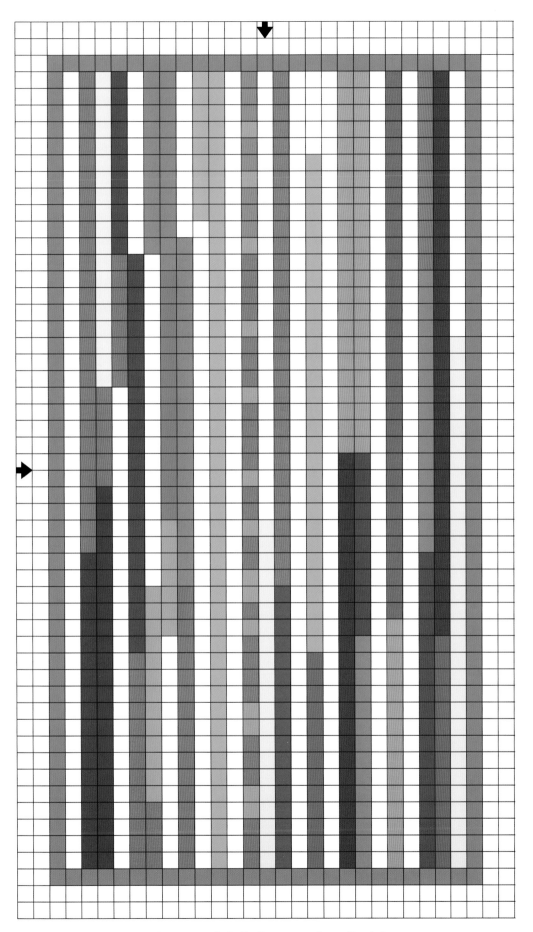

Rags and Silk Evening Bag (body)
(project instructions appear on page 43)

Rags and Silk Evening Bag

I used two of my favorite materials for this purse: osnaburg fabric and recycled sari silk ribbons. The torn strips of osnaburg create a wonderful fringe that gives this evening clutch a fibrous look that pairs well with touches of vibrant silk color. Recycled sari silk strips add a rich contrast to the coarseness of the osnaburg. This bag is a great addition to a casual outfit or something more elegant.

TECHNIQUES FOR THIS PROJECT

Preparing a Square or Rectangular Base

Framing the Base

Linear Locker Hooking

Sewing in Tails

Glued Lining

MATERIALS LIST

3.3 mesh canvas

30 yds. (27.4m) of 1" (2.5cm) osnaburg fabric strips

30 yds. (27.4m) of 1"–1½" (2.5cm–4cm) recycled sari silk strips

10 yds. (9.1m) of ½" (1.5cm) rayon seam binding

Locking medium (I recommend cream colored cotton twine for the osnaburg portions and black yarn for the sari silk)

Locker hook

Tapestry needle

Scissors

Permanent adhesive

Small clutch-style purse

1 Cut a piece of rug canvas to fit your purse—my project uses a piece of canvas 31 squares wide and 54 squares tall. Fold over the edges of the canvas by creasing the rows indicated by the gray area in the pattern on page 41 (see Preparing a Square or Rectangular Base on pages 17–18).

2 Frame the edges with rayon seam binding (see Framing the Base on pages 20–21).

3 Locker hook the canvas using the linear method (see Linear Locker Hooking on page 26). You can follow the pattern on page 41 or randomly alternate osnaburg and silk strips to give your purse a unique look.

4 Sew in all of the fabric and locking medium tails (see Sewing in Tails on pages 30–31).

5 Attach the locker-hooked canvas to your purse with permanent adhesive as if you were gluing on a lining (see Glued Lining on page 32). Let the glue dry completely.

MAKE IT FROM SCRATCH

Instead of using a purchased purse for this design, you can create your own purse by sewing a lining and attaching it to a purse frame. Going this route makes the project more complex, but also more uniquely yours!

Vineyard Leaves Belt

This belt is the perfect way to display the ruched frame technique. It's one of the easiest projects in the book and it can be finished quickly. And, best of all, it looks great with a wide variety of tops—it adds that perfect, colorful accent to an outfit. You can wear it with something casual or use it to dress up a simple outfit. Try making it wider for a more stylish look. You can use silk as shown or other light-weight fabrics in your favorite colors.

TECHNIQUES FOR THIS PROJECT

Preparing a Square or Rectangular Base

Framing the Base

Spiral Locker Hooking

Straight Ruched Frames

Sewing in Tails

Embellishing Projects

MATERIALS LIST (FOR A 31½" (80CM) BELT—A LONGER BELT WILL REQUIRE MORE MATERIALS)

5 mesh canvas

9 yds. (8.2m) of ½" (1.5cm) burgundy ribbon

16 yds. (14.6m) of ½" (1.5cm) mauve ribbon

16 yds. (14.6m) of 1" (2.5cm) recycled sari silk strips

Heavy wool yarn for ruched frame padding

Locking medium (I recommend a sturdy yarn or cotton twine in black, or in a color that matches the fabric strips)

Decorative clasp

Locker hook

Tapestry needle

Scissors

Sewing needle

Sturdy thread

Permanent adhesive (optional)

1 Cut a piece of rug canvas that is 16 squares tall and long enough to comfortably fit around your waist. The belt shown here is 168 squares long. Fold over the edges of the canvas by creasing the rows indicated by the gray area in the pattern on page 46 (see Preparing a Square or Rectangular Base on pages 17–18).

2 Frame the edges of the canvas with burgundy ribbon (see Framing the Base on pages 20–21).

3 Locker hook one round around the outer edge of the canvas using mauve ribbon and the spiral technique (see Spiral Locker Hooking on page 26).

4 Stitch on the heavy wool yarn to pad the ruched frame area of the belt (see Straight Ruched Frames on pages 28–29).

5 Cover the padded frame with silk strips following the chart on page 46.

6 Sew in the tails of fabric, locking medium and ruched frame padding (see Sewing in Tails on pages 30–31).

7 Attach the decorative clasp using a sewing needle and sturdy thread (see Embellishing Projects on page 34). If you like, secure the sturdy thread by adding drops of permanent adhesive.

CUSTOMIZE THE CLASP

The leaf clasp shown here looks great against the silk in this design, but you can use any clasp you like. Use more than one clasp if you make a wider belt.

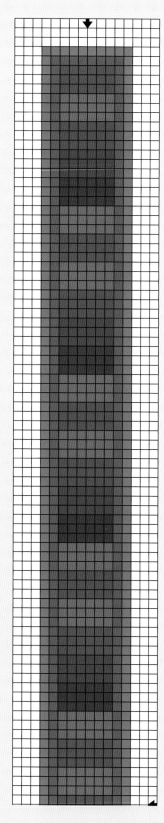

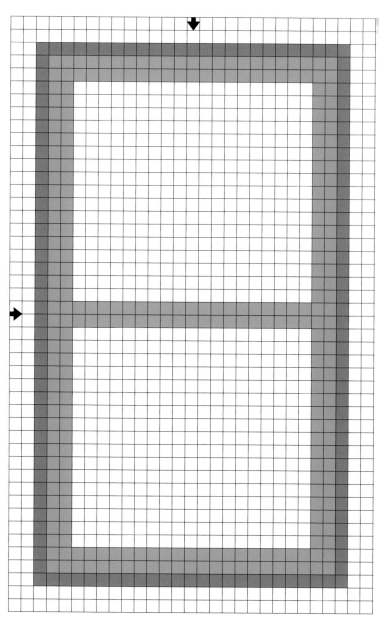

Farmer's Market Tote Bag (side)

(project instructions appear on page 49)

Vineyard Leaves Belt

(project instructions appear on page 45)

This chart shows half of the belt. To complete the belt, work from top to bottom, then repeat the chart from bottom to top.

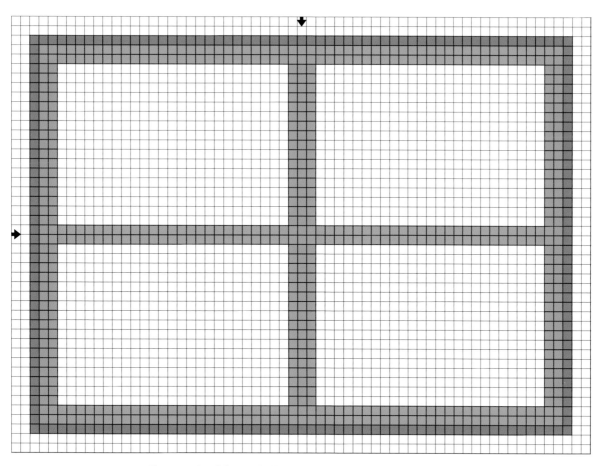

Farmer's Market Tote Bag (front and back)

(project instructions appear on page 49)

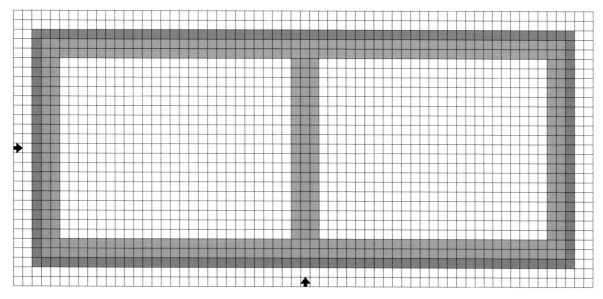

Farmer's Market Tote Bag (bottom)

(project instructions appear on page 49)

Farmer's Market Tote Bag

A sturdy tote bag is always great to have on hand for treks to the market, picnics or a trip to the beach. The need to pack a few things for a casual meal was the inspiration for this tote bag; it can carry just what you need—whether it's a delicious lunch or just refreshments and a beach towel. This project requires minimal locker hooking and some assembly. You can create your own design by filling in the panels, customizing the colors and embellishing it with your own accents.

TECHNIQUES FOR THIS PROJECT

Preparing a Square or Rectangular Base

Spiral Locker Hooking

Sewing in Tails

Assembling Projects

Framing the Base

Embellishing Projects

MATERIALS LIST

3.75 mesh canvas

20 yds. (18.3m) of ¾" (2cm) chartreuse cotton fabric strips

95 yds. (86.9m) of ½" (1.5cm) turquoise cotton flannel strips

Locking medium (I recommend a sturdy yarn or cotton twine in black, or in a color that matches the fabric strips)

Rattan purse handles

3 leaf embellishments (see pages 50-51)

Red lead-free acrylic spray paint

Locker hook

Tapestry needle

Scissors

Permanent adhesive (optional)

1 Cut five pieces of canvas: two pieces 63 squares wide and 46 squares tall for the front and back of the tote, two pieces 29 squares wide and 46 squares tall for the sides of the tote, and a piece 63 squares wide and 29 squares tall for the bottom of the tote.

Paint each piece of canvas with spray paint. Use two coats of paint on each side of each piece of canvas. Let the paint dry completely. Fold over the edges of each piece of canvas by creasing the row indicated by the gray area in the patterns on pages 46-47 (see Preparing a Square or Rectangular Base on pages 17-18).

2 Locker hook each piece following the patterns on pages 46-47 using the spiral method and turquoise flannel strips (see Spiral Locker Hooking on page 26).

3 Sew in all fabric and locking medium tails (see Sewing in Tails on pages 30-31).

4 Whipstitch the front and back pieces to the sides with chartreuse cottons strips (see Assembling Projects on page 33). Stitch the bottom piece to the front, back and sides.

5 Frame the top edge of the tote using chartreuse cotton fabric strips (see Framing the Base on pages 20-21).

6 Sew or glue on the leaf embellishments or another embellishment of your choice (see Embellishing Projects on page 34).

7 Sew the handles to the front and back of the tote using turquoise flannel strips as shown at left.

LEAF EMBELLISHMENTS

You can trace the designs I've included here or create your own templates to give your leaf embellishments a unique look.

TECHNIQUES FOR THIS PROJECT

Preparing a Shaped Base

Framing the Base

Free Form Locker Hooking

Shaped Ruched Frames

Sewing in Tails

Self-Adhesive Fabric Lining

Embellishing Projects

MATERIALS LIST

5 mesh canvas

5 yds.–8 yds. (4.6m–7.3m) of ½" (1.5cm) chartreuse cotton fabric strips (small leaf: 5 yds. [4.6m]; medium leaf: 5 yds. [4.6m]; large leaf: 8 yds. [7.3m])

6yds.–8 yds. (5.5m–7.3m) of ½" (1.5cm) turquoise cotton flannel strips (small leaf: 6 yds. [5.5m]; medium leaf: 7 yds. [6.4m]; large leaf: 8 yds. [7.3m])

Medium to heavy wool yarn for ruched frame padding

Locking medium (I recommend a sturdy yarn or cotton twine in black, or in a color that matches the fabric strips)

Self-adhesive fabric (optional)

Locker hook

Tapestry needle

Permanent marker

Scissors

Pinback (optional)

Sewing needle (optional)

Thread (optional)

Permanent adhesive (optional)

1 Trace your chosen leaf design onto canvas. Cut along the traced lines, then secure the edges with permanent adhesive (see Preparing a Shaped Base on page 18). Allow the glue to dry completely.

2 Frame the edges of the canvas with turquoise flannel (see Framing the Base on pages 20–21).

3 Use turquoise flannel and the free form method to locker hook the outline and center line of the design (see Free Form Locker Hooking on page 27).

4 Stitch on the medium to heavy wool yarn to pad the ruched frame areas of the leaf (see Shaped Ruched Frames on page 29).

5 Cover the padded frame with chartreuse cotton fabric strips.

6 Sew in all fabric and locking medium tails (see Sewing in Tails on pages 30–31).

7 If desired, line the back of the leaf with self-adhesive fabric (see Self-Adhesive Fabric Lining on page 32).

8 If you wish to permanently attach your leaf embellishment, you can sew it on to a project or attach it with permanent adhesive. To make a removable embellishment, attach a pinback to the leaf with either stitching or glue (see Embellishing Projects on page 34).

Leaf Embellishments (small)

(copy at 133% for full-sized template)

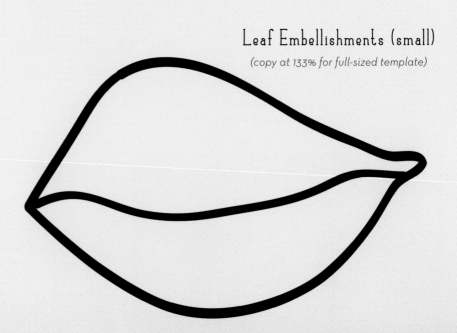

Leaf Embellishments (medium and large)
(Copy at 133% for full-sized template)

Adding Up

Don't just use these leaves on the Farmer's Market Tote. Pair them with the Floral Accents on page 52 or use them on other projects, too!

Floral Accents

Whether you use mesh canvas or linen burlap, you can create accents in just about any shape. In my opinion, flowers are always a welcome embellishment, so I chose them to be the theme for this project. They make great accents on sweaters, tote bags or hats. These simple floral designs are featured here in three different sizes, but try customizing yours by drawing your own template or tracing designs that catch your eye. Experiment with different colors and materials, by pulling up fringe for centers or by wrapping the edges with contrasting narrow ribbon. The possibilities really are endless.

TECHNIQUES FOR THIS PROJECT

Preparing a Shaped Base

Framing the Base

Free Form Locker Hooking

Sewing in Tails

Embellishing Projects

Self-Adhesive Fabric Lining

MATERIALS LIST

Linen burlap, 5 mesh canvas or 6 mesh canvas

4 yds.–12 yds. (3.7m–11m) of ½" (1.5cm) wide decorative looping material; try cotton fabric, silk ribbon, yarn and more

2 yds.–4 yds. (1.8m–3.7m) of framing material; try yarn, silk ribbon or fabric strips

Locking medium

Embellishments such as painted wood accents, antique buttons or beads

Self-adhesive fabric

Pinback (optional)

Locker hook

Tapestry needle

Sewing needle and thread

Tracing paper and pen

Permanent marker

Scissors

Permanent adhesive

1 Trace a template on page 54 onto canvas or linen burlap. Follow the steps for your chosen base in Preparing a Shaped Base on page 19.

2 Frame the edges of your base (see Framing the Base on pages 20–21).

3 Locker hook using the free form method to fill in the flower as desired (see Free Form Locker Hooking on page 27). You can leave a blank space in the middle for a large embellishment, or you can leave areas of your base exposed if you wish. Change colors and materials as you work if you desire. Pull up big loops, small loops, or a combination of loop sizes to create different looks. If you're not using an embellishment in the center of your flower, I suggest using a novelty yarn in the center of the flower.

4 Sew in the fabric and locking medium tails on the flower (see Sewing in Tails on pages 30–31). You can just clip the ends on the back of the piece short instead of sewing them in if you prefer since the loops will be secured with fabric backing.

5 Attach the embellishments of your choice to the flower by either sewing or gluing them on (see Embellishing Projects on page 34).

6 Line the back of the flower with self-adhesive fabric (see Self-Adhesive Fabric Lining on page 32). Attach a pinback if desired.

Floral Accents (small,
medium and large)
(Copy at 133% for full-sized template)
(project instructions appear on page 53)

*Add a pinback to your Floral Accent to
turn it into a brooch you can wear on a
jacket, bag or hat!*

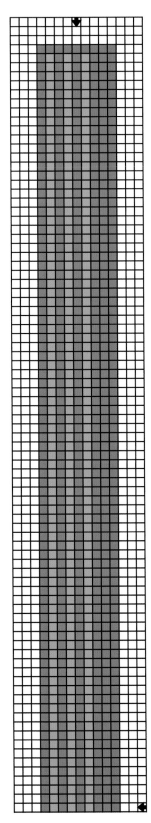

Bolero Sweater with Loopy Collar and Cuffs (collar)

(project instructions appear on page 57)

This chart shows half of the collar. To complete the collar, work from top to bottom, then repeat the chart from bottom to top.

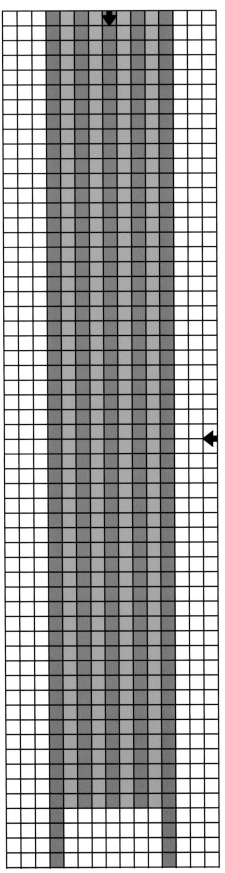

Bolero Sweater with Loopy Collar and Cuffs (cuffs)

(project instructions appear on page 57)

Bolero Sweater with Loopy Collar and Cuffs

This design makes the most of a thick-and-thin yarn, giving this simple bolero sweater a fun and stylish faux fur look. You can use this idea for any sweater or jacket in your wardrobe—just measure the area you want to cover and add enough canvas to fold over and frame the pieces. To make this design work you have to alternate loop lengths. Every other row has extra-long loops, and the rows in between have shorter loops to balance the look and give the long loops enough space to fluff up.

TECHNIQUES FOR THIS PROJECT

Preparing a Square or Rectangular Base

Framing the Base

Linear Locker Hooking

Locker Hooking in the Round

Sewing in Tails

Embellishing Projects

MATERIALS LIST

6 mesh canvas

140 yds. (128m) of olive green thick-and-thin yarn

16 yds. (14.6m) of olive rayon seam binding

2 vintage buttons

Locker hook

Tapestry needle

Sewing needle

Thread

Scissors

Permanent fabric adhesive

1 Cut three pieces of canvas: one piece for the collar and two pieces for the cuffs. For the sweater shown here I cut one piece 173 squares wide and 15 squares tall for the collar, and two pieces 58 squares wide and 15 squares tall for the cuffs. You can customize the size of your canvas pieces to fit your sweater. Fold over the edges of each piece of canvas by creasing the row indicated by the gray area in the patterns on page 55 (see Preparing a Square or Rectangular Base on pages 17–18).

2 For the collar, frame the edges of the canvas with rayon seam binding (see Framing the Base on pages 20–21). You can make a normal frame that covers just the edge of the canvas, or you can create a wider frame like I did on this project by whipstitching over two squares at the edge while framing.

3 Locker hook the collar working in the linear method (see Linear Locker Hooking on page 26). Start by hooking a row of long loops. Pull up loops that start at $^3/_4$" (2cm) tall near the end of the collar. As you near the center of the collar begin pulling up longer loops—up to $1^1/_2$" (4cm) long around the center; work back down to smaller loops as you work toward the other end. Locker hook the next row with shorter loops—about $1/_2$" (1.5cm) long. Continue alternating rows of long loops and short loops to finish the collar. You don't need to use locking medium with the longer loops, but for the $1/_2$" (1.5cm), use the thick-and-thin yarn for both the loops and locking medium.

4 Apply a light coat of fabric adhesive on the back of the collar to secure the loops. Let the glue dry completely.

5 To make the cuffs you will be working in the round (see Locker Hooking in the Round on page 27). Overlap four squares of canvas to make the canvas pieces circular and locker hook each cuff following the pattern on page 55. Alternate the length of each row of loops—the long rows should be $^5/_8$" (1.5cm) long, and the short rows $1/_4$" (6mm) long. Use the thick-and-thin yarn for both the loops and locking medium. Frame the edges of each cuff with rayon seam binding. Sew in all yarn tails (see Sewing in Tails on pages 30–31).

6 Using a sewing needle and matching thread, hand stitch the cuffs and collar onto the sweater. Sew on the vintage buttons at each end of the collar (see Embellishing Projects on page 34).

Dahlia Ring Bearer's Pillow

This adorable ring bearer's pillow can be customized to match the color scheme of any wedding. It also makes a beautiful accent pillow. This design juxtaposes soft and silky textures with fibrous ones. The silky blossom set against the linen burlap is a beautiful contrast. This is a rather simple design, but once completed the pillow looks pretty and sumptuous.

TECHNIQUES FOR THIS PROJECT

Preparing a Square or Rectangular Base

Spiral Locker Hooking

Self-Adhesive Fabric Lining

MATERIALS LIST

Linen burlap

$2\frac{1}{2}$ yds. (2.3m) of 7mm wide medium pink silk ribbon

$2\frac{1}{2}$ yds. (2.3m) of 13mm wide dark pink silk ribbon

9 yds. (8.2m) of $\frac{5}{8}$" (1.5cm) wide pale pink silk ribbon

$1\frac{1}{2}$ yds (1.4m) of 13mm wide medium pink silk ribbon

20" (51cm) of 13mm wide sheer metallic ribbon

Metallic fabric paint

7" x 7" (18cm x 18cm) piece of self-adhesive fabric

9" x 9" (23cm x 23cm) pillow form

Crushed velvet

Locker hook

Tapestry needle

Sewing needle

Thread

Tracing paper

Iron-on transfer pen

Iron

Scissors

Permanent adhesive

Paintbrush

1 Cut the linen burlap to $10\frac{1}{2}$" x $10\frac{1}{2}$" (26.5cm x 26.5cm). Use a steam iron to press under a $\frac{3}{4}$" (2cm) seam allowance on each side (see Preparing a Square or Rectangular Base on pages 17–18).

2 Paint a $\frac{1}{2}$" (1.5cm) wide frame around the pressed edge of the canvas. Allow the paint to dry completely.

3 Using a tapestry needle and 7mm wide pink ribbon, follow the pattern on page 60 to stitch two frames inside the painted frame.

4 If you like, transfer the dahlia design from page 60 to the linen burlap. I suggest using an iron-on transfer pen for easy transfer—follow the manufacturer's instructions.

5 Locker hook the dahlia design, starting at the center of the design and working outward using the spiral method (see Spiral Locker Hooking on page 26). As you complete each round, adjust the loops by twisting them just a bit so they look like flower petals. Begin with 7mm medium pink ribbon; when it runs out, work one round with 13mm dark pink ribbon, then switch to $\frac{5}{8}$" (1.5cm) pale pink ribbon.

6 Cut two 20" (51cm) lengths of ribbon for the bow, one from the 13mm wide medium pink ribbon and one from the 13mm wide sheer metallic ribbon. Take one stitch through the burlap close to the flower with both ribbons, then tie them into a bow. Trim the ribbon ends to the length you prefer.

STOP AND SMELL THE FLOWERS

Instead of using a pillow form, try filling the pillow like an oversized sachet with a subtle potpourri of flower petals or lavender.

7 Line the back of the dahlia with self-adhesive fabric (see Self-Adhesive Fabric Lining on page 32).

8 To create a decorative edge, on the wrong side of the piece of locker-hooked burlap, glue pieces of 13mm wide medium pink ribbon to the very edge of the burlap so that they extend past the burlap.

9 Cut a 10½" x 10½" (26.5cm x 26.5cm) piece of crushed velvet for the pillow backing. Fold a seam allowance around the edge of the velvet to match the size of the velvet piece to the size of the linen burlap. Press the seam allowance down on the wrong side of the velvet. Hand stitch the backing to the burlap on three sides. Insert the pillow form and finish stitching the velvet to the burlap.

Dahlia Ring Bearer's Pillow
(copy at 133% for full-sized template)

(project instructions appear on page 59)

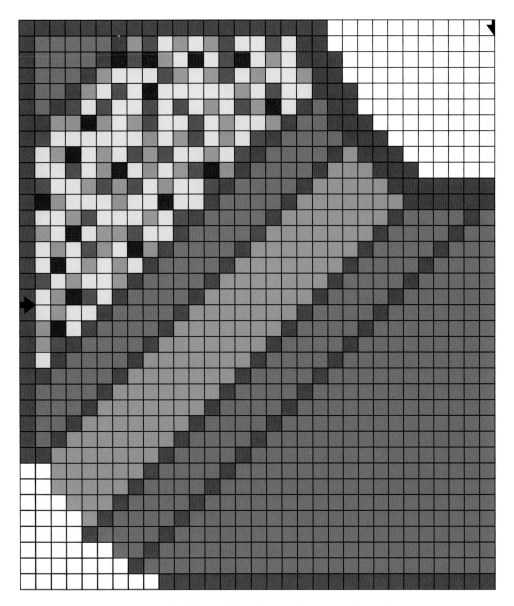

Tropical Moon Tote Bag (front and back)

(project instructions appear on page 63)

*This chart shows half of the pattern. To complete the pattern, work from
left to right, then repeat the chart from right to left.*

Tropical Moon Tote Bag

This tote uses the new ruched frame technique along with a bright turquoise silk to create stunning diagonal accents. It also teaches you how to easily assemble curved pieces. This unique locker-hooked design can be adapted to make a deeper or larger bag once you've mastered these techniques. A great accent that will definitely ramp up the fun look of this bag is more fringe. Try silk ribbons and novelty yarn to add more texture.

TECHNIQUES FOR THIS PROJECT

Preparing a Square or Rectangular Base

Preparing a Shaped Base

Spiral Locker Hooking

Linear Locker Hooking

Straight Ruched Frames

Sewing in Tails

Assembling Projects

Framing the Base

MATERIALS LIST

3.75 mesh canvas

20 yds. (18.3m) of ³/₄" (2cm) turquoise recycled sari silk strips

35 yds. (32m) of ³/₄" (2cm) multicolor print fabric strips

80 yds. (73.2m) of ³/₄" (2cm) blue-green cotton fabric strips

85 yds. (77.7m) of ½" (1.5cm) brown flannel fabric strips

12 yds. (11m) of ½" (1.5cm) slate blue rayon seam binding

Heavy wool yarn for ruched frame padding

Locking medium (I recommend a sturdy yarn or cotton twine in black, or in a color that matches the fabric strips)

2 round rattan purse handles

Locker hook

Tapestry needle

Scissors

Permanent adhesive

1 Cut three pieces of canvas: two pieces 62 squares wide and 36 squares tall for the front and back of the bag and a piece 136 squares wide and 20 squares tall for the sides and bottom of the bag. Fold over the edges of canvas piece for the side and bottom of the bag by creasing the fourth row of canvas on all sides (see Preparing a Square or Rectangular Base on pages 17–18).

2 Using the template on page 61, cut curves at the bottom corners of the pieces of canvas for the front and back of the bag. Secure the edges of these pieces of canvas with glue (see Preparing a Shaped Base on page 18).

3 Using brown flannel strips, locker hook one row around the edge of the front and back pieces of the bag; work in a spiral (see Spiral Locker Hooking on page 26).

4 Using the linear method, locker hook the brown diagonal lines on the front and back pieces of the bag (see Linear Locker Hooking on page 26). Locker hook the blue-green and multicolor print portions of the front and back of the purse as well, again using the linear method.

5 Stitch on the heavy wool yarn to pad the ruched frame areas on the front and back of the bag (see Straight Ruched Frames on pages 28–29).

6 Cover the padded frames with turquoise silk strips following the chart on page 61.

7 Next, switch to the canvas for the sides and bottom of the bag. Locker hook one round around the outer edge of the canvas using brown flannel and the spiral technique.

8 Stitch on the heavy wool yarn to pad the ruched frame area of the sides and bottom of the bag. Cover the padded frame with multicolor print strips.

9 Sew in the fabric and locking medium tails on each piece of the bag (see Sewing in Tails on pages 30–31).

10 Whipstitch the strip that makes up the sides and bottom of the bag to both the front and back of the bag using rayon seam binding (see Assembling Projects on page 33).

11 Frame the top edge of the bag with rayon seam binding (see Framing the Base on pages 20–21).

12 Attach rattan handles to the front and back of the bag by whipstitching them on with brown flannel strips. If desired, embellish the bag with a fringe of fabric strips.

Harlequin Bracelet

I was experimenting with creating wide bracelets when I made this design. As I worked, I found that the nice thing about working on linen burlap is that you can easily create a wide variety of designs on it. While this is a simple design, you can get as creative as you want and design detailed swirls or even monograms. For this design, the vintage glass buttons add the perfect touch for a closure. Try this bracelet design in different colors with a variety of closures, like buttons, a clasp, or just a simple ribbon tie-on.

TECHNIQUES FOR THIS PROJECT

Preparing a Shaped Base

Framing the Base

Free Form Locker Hooking

Sewing in Tails

Embellishing Projects

MATERIALS

Linen burlap

8 yds. (7.3m) of ¾" (2cm) recycled sari silk strips in multiple colors

2 yds. (1.8m) of ½" (1.5cm) magenta rayon seam binding

Locking medium

2 small buttons

Seed beads

Locker hook

Tapestry needle

Beading needle

Thread

Permanent adhesive

Scissors

Tracing paper

Iron-on transfer pen

Iron

1 Copy and enlarge the bracelet design below. The enlarging instructions are for a small bracelet, but you can add length to the design to size it as you wish. Transfer the design to the linen burlap. I suggest using an iron-on transfer pen for easy transfer—following the manufacturer's instructions, transfer the design onto the linen burlap piece using tracing paper and an iron-on transfer pen (see Preparing a Shaped Base on pages 18–19).

2 Apply a thin line of glue along the outline of the design and let it dry. Cut out the design just outside the glued outline. Frame the edges of the bracelet with seam binding (see Framing the Base on pages 20–21).

3 Locker hook the zigzag design inside the bracelet using the free form method (see Free Form Locker Hooking on page 27). Fill in the areas on each side of the zigzag line using the free form method.

4 Sew in the fabric and locking medium tails (see Sewing in Tails on pages 30–31). Attach two buttons to one end of the bracelet (see Embellishing Projects on page 34). Use a beading needle, thread and matching seed beads to create loops opposite the buttons (see the photo below for guidance). Secure the knots in the thread with a tiny drop of glue.

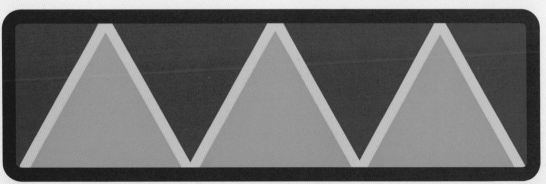

65

Copy at 133% for full-sized template

Floppy-Eared Bunny Basket

A few easy embellishments turn this simple basket into a sweet, floppy-eared bunny. It's great fun for Easter egg hunting or just for a whimsical bit of décor. You can alter the colors to make your bunny lighter, darker or jelly-bean colored. You can even use novelty yarn or unspun mohair to make the bunny fluffy and fun.

TECHNIQUES FOR THIS PROJECT

Preparing a Square or Rectangular Base

Preparing a Shaped Base

Framing the Base

Spiral Locker Hooking

Locker Hooking in the Round

Linear Locker Hooking

Sewing in Tails

Assembling Projects

MATERIALS

5 mesh canvas

70 yds. (64m) of ½" (1.5cm) natural muslin cotton fabric strips

15 yds. (13.7m) of ivory heavy cotton/wool blend yarn

15 yds. (13.7m) of sable heavy cotton/wool blend yarn

16½ yds. (15.1m) of ½" (1.5cm) sable rayon seam binding

1 yd. (.9m) of ½" (1.5cm) pink velvet ribbon

Locking medium

Locker hook

Tapestry needle

Scissors

Fast-drying permanent adhesive

1 Cut five pieces of canvas: one piece 81 squares wide and 30 squares tall for the body of the basket, one piece 26 squares wide and 26 squares tall for the bottom of the basket, one piece 62 squares wide and 10 squares tall for the basket handle and two pieces for the ears using the template on page 68. Fold over the edges of each piece of canvas except the ears by creasing the rows indicated by the gray areas in the patterns on pages 68–69 (see Preparing a Square or Rectangular Base on pages 17–18). Secure the edges of the ears with glue (see Preparing a Shaped Base on page 18).

2 Frame the edges of the ears with sable seam binding (see Framing the Base on pages 20–21). You can make a normal frame that covers just the edge of the ears, or you can create a wider frame like I did on this project by whipstitching over two squares at the edge while framing.

3 Locker hook each ear following the pattern on page 68, using cotton/wool blend yarns and the spiral method (see Spiral Locker Hooking on page 26).

4 Locker hook the muzzle on the face with ivory yarn and the spiral method. Once the muzzle is complete, finish the basket body by working in the round (see Locker Hooking in the Round on page 27). Overlap four squares of canvas to make the canvas piece circular and locker hook the basket body following the pattern on page 68.

5 Locker hook the bottom of the basket by following the pattern on page 68 and using the spiral technique. Locker hook the basket's handle by following the pattern on page 69 and using the linear method (see Linear Locker Hooking on page 26). Leave two rows of canvas unhooked at each end of the handle.

6 Before assembling the basket, embellish the bunny's face. Following the chart on page 68, make the bunny's eyes by making two stitches for each eye with the sable seam binding. To create the bunny's nose and mouth, make two horizontal, parallel stitches with the pink velvet ribbon. Join the two stitches with one vertical stitch that pulls the horizontal stitches inward.

7 Sew in the fabric and locking medium tails on each piece of the basket (see Sewing in Tails on pages 30–31). Whipstitch the basket body to the bottom of the basket (see Assembling Projects on page 33).

8 Frame the top edge of the basket body and the long edges of the handle with rayon seam binding. Stitch the ears and handle to the basket body with cotton/wool blend yarn. Sew in any remaining tails.

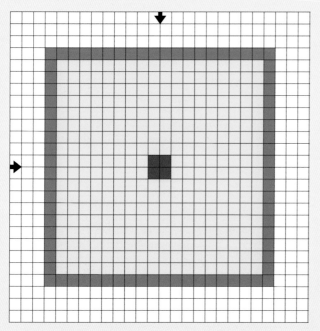

Floppy-Eared Bunny Basket (bottom)

(project instructions start on page 67)

Floppy-Eared Bunny Basket (ear)

(project instructions start on page 67)

Copy at 200% for full-sized template

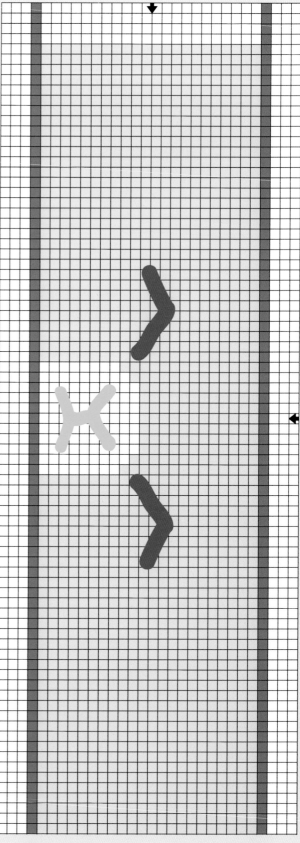

Floppy-Eared Bunny Basket (body)

(project instructions start on page 67)

Copy at 125% for full-sized embroidery template for the eyes, nose and mouth

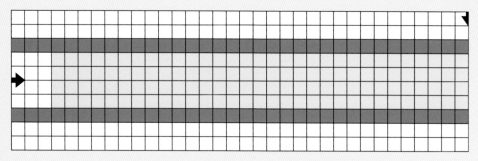

Floppy-Eared Bunny Basket (handle)

(project instructions start on page 67)

This chart shows half of the pattern. To complete the pattern, work from left to right, then repeat the chart from right to left.

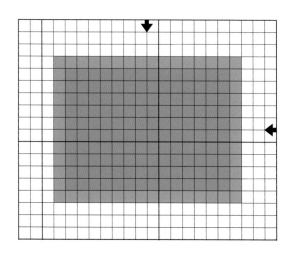

Floral Business Card Holder (bottom)

(project instructions appear on page 71)

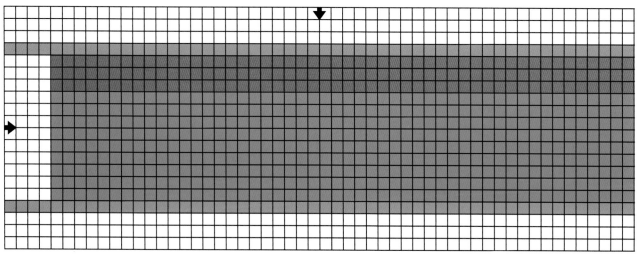

Floral Business Card Holder (body)

(project instructions appear on page 71)

GREGORY BERTOLINI PHOTOGRAPHY

208 West 23rd St #1511
New York NY 10011

917.750.6952

gbertolini@earthlink.net

Floral Business Card Holder

Locker hooking a small project for a gift is a very rewarding experience—this small basket is a great example. It can be locker hooked fairly quickly and you can color coordinate the colors to match décor, or choose the recipient's favorites. While it makes for a whimsical business card holder on a desk or counter, you can fill this with potpourri or with treats to give as a gift. Get creative with the embellishments! I chose a pretty velvety rose accent, but you can choose to add beads, tie a bow on or even add a sprinkling of glitter.

TECHNIQUES FOR THIS PROJECT

Preparing a Square or Rectangular Base

Locker Hooking in the Round

Spiral Locker Hooking

Sewing in Tails

Assembling Projects

Framing the Base

Embellishing Projects

MATERIALS LIST

5 mesh canvas

24 yds. (21.9m) of ½" (1.5cm) blue cotton fabric strips

12 yds. (11m) of ½" (1.5cm) magenta rayon seam binding

Locking medium (I recommend a sturdy yarn or cotton twine in black, or in a color that matches the fabric strips)

Embellishment such as a velvety flower

Locker hook

Tapestry needle

Permanent adhesive

Scissors

Ruler

1 Cut two pieces of mesh canvas: one piece 54 squares wide and 20 squares tall for the body of the basket, and one piece 22 squares wide and 18 squares tall for the bottom of the basket. Fold over the edges of each piece of canvas by creasing the rows indicated by the gray areas in the patterns on page 69 (see Preparing a Square or Rectangular Base on pages 17-18).

2 To make the basket body you will be working in the round (see Locker Hooking in the Round on page 27). Overlap four squares of canvas to make the canvas piece circular. Start at the bottom working with blue cotton and switch to magenta seam binding when indicated by the pattern on page 69. When working with the magenta seam binding pull up long loops—¾"-1" (2cm-2.5cm).

3 Locker hook the bottom of the basket following the pattern on page 69 and using the spiral technique (see Spiral Locker Hooking on page 26).

4 Sew in the fabric and locking medium tails on each piece of the basket (see Sewing in Tails on pages 30-31).

5 Whipstitch the basket body to the bottom of the basket (see Assembling Projects on page 33).

6 Frame the top edge of the basket body with rayon seam binding (see Framing the Base on pages 20-21). Attach the flower or embellishment of your choice with permanent adhesive (see Embellishing Projects on page 34).

Meadowlands Fibers Purse

This purse is created on a molded mesh frame that gives it its wonderful shape. The textured look of this purse is created by locker hooking a rich novelty yarn layered with cotton flannel print strips. You can easily create this look in your own favorite colors, or change the handle length for a custom fit.

TECHNIQUES FOR THIS PROJECT

Spiral Locker Hooking

Linear Locker Hooking

Locker Hooking with Multiple Materials

Sewing in Tails

Assembling Projects

Framing the Base

Preparing a Square or Rectangular Base

Straight Ruched Frames

MATERIALS LIST

Plastic mesh purse frame

3.75 mesh canvas

65 yds. (59.4m) of 1/2"–3/4" (1.5cm–2cm) multicolor print flannel fabric strips

62 yds. (56.7m) of multicolor fringed novelty yarn

10 yds. (9.1m) of 3/4"–1" (2cm–2.5cm) recycled sari silk strips in multiple colors

7 yds. (6.4m) of 1/2"–3/4" (1.5cm–2cm) solid flannel fabric strips

10 yds. (9.1m) of 1/2" (1.5cm) rayon seam binding

Heavy wool yarn for ruched frame padding

Locking medium (I recommend a sturdy yarn or cotton twine in black, or in a color that matches the fabric strips)

2 1⅝" (4cm) buttons

Locker hook

Tapestry needle

Sewing needle

Thread

Scissors

1 Locker hook three rows around the edges of both halves of the purse frame using sold flannel fabric strips; work in a spiral (see Spiral Locker Hooking on page 26).

2 Using the linear method, locker hook an additional three rows at the bottom of each half of the purse frame with solid flannel for a total of six rows on each half at the bottom of the bag (see Linear Locker Hooking on page 26). Where the purse frame curves it can have uneven, slightly larger squares. If the canvas doesn't look filled in by the rows you've just created, locker hook additional rows on the bottom of each piece between existing rows to fill in as needed.

3 Using strips of patterned flannel held together with novelty yarn, locker hook the rest of each side of the purse frame (see Locker Hooking with Multiple Materials on page 24).

4 Sew in the fabric and locking medium tails on each piece of the bag (see Sewing in Tails on pages 30–31). Whipstitch the pieces of the purse frame together (see Assembling Projects on page 33). Frame the top edge of the bag with rayon seam binding (see Framing the Base on pages 20–21).

5 Cut a piece of rug canvas that is 12 squares wide and 86 squares long. Fold over the edges of the canvas by creasing the rows indicated by the gray area in the pattern below (see Preparing a Square or Rectangular Base on pages 17–18). Frame the edges of the canvas with rayon seam binding.

6 Locker hook one round around the outer edge of the canvas using flannel strips and the spiral technique. Stitch on heavy wool yarn to pad the ruched frame area of the handle (see Straight Ruched Frames on pages 28–29). Cover the padded frame with silk strips following the chart below. The chart below shows half of the pattern. To complete the pattern, work from left to right, then repeat the chart from right to left.

7 Sew in the tails of fabric, locking medium and ruched frame padding. Attach the handle to the purse. Use a sewing needle and thread to attach button accents at each side.

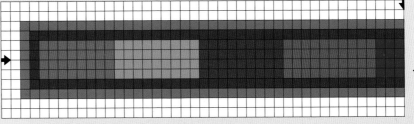

Oh, Christmas Tree! Ornament

One of my favorite things to do is decorate for the holidays. It is so much fun to have ornaments and other holiday décor items throughout the house. You can hang ornaments on kitchen cabinet handles and even bedroom doors. It's incredibly charming to open a cabinet door with a beautiful ornament hanging off the knob to grab a coffee or tea cup. Try different color schemes to create a whimsical mix of holiday colors and designs. It's a great way to introduce some holiday cheer.

TECHNIQUES FOR THIS PROJECT

- Preparing a Shaped Base
- Framing the Base
- Free Form Locker Hooking
- Sewing in Tails
- Embellishing Projects
- Self-Adhesive Fabric Lining

MATERIALS LIST

- 3.75 mesh canvas or 5 mesh canvas
- 16 yds. (14.6m) of 1/2"–3/4" (1.5cm–2cm) green ribbon or cotton fabric strips (thinner strips for 5 mesh canvas or thicker strips for 3.75 mesh canvas)
- 5 yds. (4.6m) of 1/2"–3/4" (1.5cm–2cm) red ribbon or cotton fabric strips (thinner strips for 5 mesh canvas or thicker strips for 3.75 mesh canvas)
- Locking medium (I recommend a sturdy yarn or cotton twine in black)
- Embellishments such as large resin beads
- Self-adhesive fabric
- Locker hook
- Tapestry needle
- Scissors
- Sewing needle
- Permanent adhesive
- Permanent marker

1 Trace the template below onto canvas. Cut out the tree and secure the edges with glue (see Preparing a Shaped Base on page 18, Finishing Sharp Corners on page 35).

2 Frame the edges of the canvas with green ribbon (see Framing the Base on pages 20–21).

3 Using the free form method, locker hook the red garland on the tree with red fabric or ribbon strips (see Free Form Locker Hooking on page 27).

4 Locker hook the background using green ribbon or fabric strips and the free form method; travel locking medium and fabric strips as needed.

5 Sew in the fabric, ribbon and locking medium tails (see Sewing in Tails on pages 30–31). Attach the bead "ornaments" to the tree by either sewing or gluing them on (see Embellishing Projects on page 34).

6 Sew a red ribbon through the top center of the ornament for hanging. Line the back of the ornament with self-adhesive fabric (see Self-Adhesive Fabric Lining on page 32).

Copy first at 200%, then at 150% for full-sized template

Ho, Ho, Ho! Santa Ornament

My mother-in-law inspired me to design this Santa ornament and I'm so glad I gave it a try. It's a good way to try using unspun mohair locks for incredible texture. If you are not comfortable using the unspun locks, you can easily create the beard with some heavy ivory wool yarn. The face looks very sweet locker hooked with wool strips, but you can also use the heavy yarn. Whatever you do, have fun creating this ornament!

TECHNIQUES FOR THIS PROJECT

Preparing a Shaped Base

Framing the Base

Linear Locker Hooking

Sewing in Tails

Self-Adhesive Fabric Lining

MATERIALS LIST

5 mesh canvas

2½ yds. (2.3m) of ½" (1.5cm) green rayon seam binding

4 yds. (3.7m) of ½" (1.5cm) red cotton fabric strips

2 yds. (1.8m) of ¼" (6mm) flesh tone wool strips

9" (23cm) of ½" (1.5cm) brown cotton fabric strips

2 yds. (1.8m) of ½" (1.5cm) ivory rayon seam binding

¼ oz. (7g) unspun ivory mohair locks

Locking medium (I recommend cream colored cotton twine for the face and beard, and black yarn for the hat)

Red glitter

1 yd. (.9m) red ribbon

Self-adhesive fabric

Locker hook

Tapestry needle

Permanent markers

Scissors

Permanent adhesive

1 Trace the template on page 78 onto canvas. Cut out the template and secure the edges with glue (see Preparing a Shaped Base on page 18).

2 Frame the edges of the canvas (see Framing the Base on pages 20–21). You can use one color to frame the canvas, or match the frame to the colors in the pattern as I did.

3 Locker hook the green part of the hat in diagonal lines using the linear method (see Linear Locker Hooking on page 26).

4 Locker hook the red part of the hat from side to side using the linear method. Locker hook the face from side to side using the linear method, switching colors as indicated by the pattern on page 78.

5 Sew in the fabric and locking medium tails (see Sewing in Tails on pages 30–31).

6 Locker hook the beard using unspun mohair or bulky ivory yarn. See the photos on page 78 for more information on working with unspun fiber.

7 Add drops of adhesive to the ornament where you'd like glitter accents. Sprinkle glitter onto the adhesive, then shake off the excess. Let the adhesive dry completely.

8 Sew a red ribbon through the top center of the ornament for hanging. Line the back of the ornament with self-adhesive fabric (see Self-Adhesive Fabric Lining on page 32).

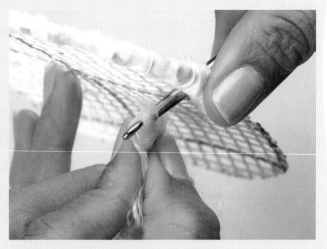

1 Fluff the unspun fiber to open it up and separate the locks a bit. Gather two to three locks and grasp them at both ends. Twist the locks together so that they will hold together during locker hooking.

2 Locker hook with the locks as you would with a fuzzy yarn. Continue to add on additional locks of fiber by twisting them in as you locker hook so the locks cling together. Take care not to run out as you work.

78

Ho, Ho, Ho! Santa Ornament

(project instructions appear on page 77)

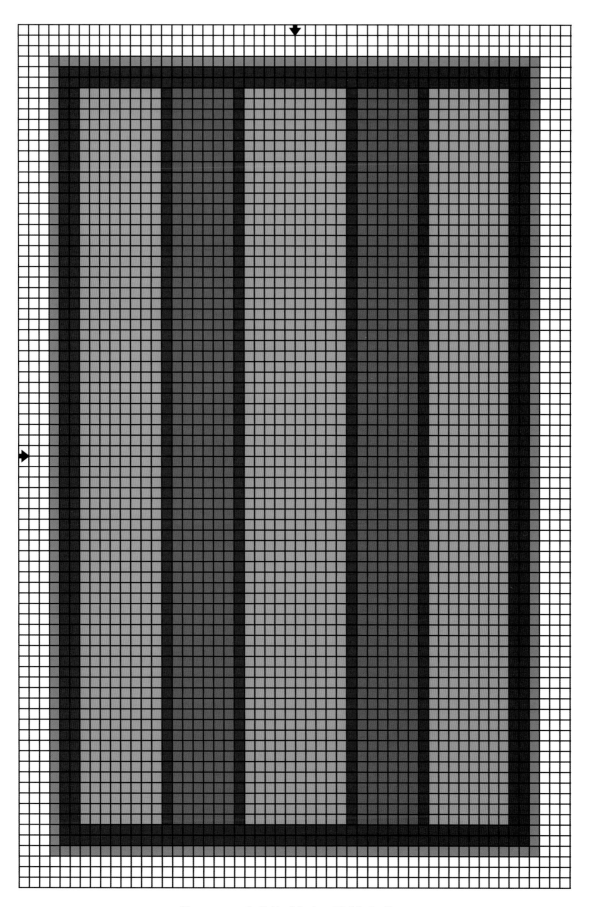

Denim and Silk Media Tablet Cover

(project instructions appear on page 81)

Denim and Silk Media Tablet Cover

This design allows you to recycle a pair of jeans and some silk remnants to create a beautiful protective cover. Whether you own a media tablet or just want a handcrafted journal cover, this is the perfect design to cover and protect precious cargo. The denim adds a retro touch to this design but you can use regular cotton fabric as well—deep indigo blue cotton would also turn out a beautiful design.

TECHNIQUES FOR THIS PROJECT

Preparing a Square or Rectangular Base

Framing the Base

Linear Locker Hooking

Straight Ruched Frames

Sewing in Tails

MATERIALS LIST

3.75 mesh canvas

32 yds. (29.3m) of ½" (1.5cm) denim strips

25 yds. (22.9.m) of ½" (1.5cm) faux suede strips

16 yds. (14.6m) of ½" (1.5cm) purple recycled sari silk strips

8 yds. (7.3m) of ½" (1.5cm) brown rayon seam binding

Heavy wool yarn for ruched frame padding

Locking medium (I recommend a sturdy yarn or cotton twine in a color that matches the fabric strips)

Fabric for lining and pockets; cut into one 11½" × 17½" (29cm × 44.5cm) piece and three 11½" × 4½" (29cm × 11.5cm) pieces

1 large button

38" (96.5cm) leather cord

Locker hook

Tapestry needle

Sewing needle

Tapestry thread

Iron

Sewing machine and thread

Scissors

Permanent fabric adhesive

1. Cut a piece of canvas 82 squares wide and 54 squares tall. Fold over the edges of the canvas by creasing the rows indicated by the gray areas in the pattern on page 79 (see Preparing a Square or Rectangular Base on pages 17–18). Transfer the pattern on page 79 to the canvas if you desire.

2. Frame the edges of the canvas with rayon seam binding (see Framing the Base on pages 20–21).

3. Using the denim strips, locker hook the frames and dividing lines of the pattern working in the linear fashion (see Linear Locker Hooking on page 26).

4. Stitch on the heavy wool yarn to pad the ruched frame areas of the cover (see Straight Ruched Frames on pages 28–29).

5. Cover the padded frame with faux suede strips and silk strips following the chart on page 79.

6. Sew in the fabric and locking medium tails (see Sewing in Tails on pages 30–31).

7. Sew the large button to one side of the cover near the edge. Sew the leather cord to the other edge of the cover directly opposite the button.

8. Turn under and stitch a ½" (1.5cm) hem on each piece of the lining fabric. Position the pieces of pocket fabric on the edges of the lining fabric and stitch them down.

9. Apply permanent fabric adhesive around the outer edge of the wrong side of the lining. Place the lining on the inside of the cover. Secure the cover and lining with clamps until the glue is completely dry.

SECURITY MEASURES

If you use a light-weight fabric for your lining and pockets, iron on a fusible interface to the fabric for extra support.

Velvet Rose Necklace

With the new techniques detailed in this book, you can create small, unique projects like this richly textured necklace. It adds an elegant touch to a casual outfit or can be the perfect accent for a special occasion. This necklace is a clear example of how you can take locker-hooked elements and incorporate other crafts, like jewelry making, to create extraordinary accessories. Try using fabric remnants left over from other projects to create your own necklace design.

TECHNIQUES FOR THIS PROJECT

Preparing a Shaped Base

Framing the Base

Free Form Locker Hooking

Spiral Locker Hooking

Shaped Ruched Frames

Sewing in Tails

Self-Adhesive Fabric Lining

MATERIALS LIST

5 mesh canvas

1½ yds. (1.4m) of ¾" (2cm) crushed velvet fabric strips

9 yds. (8.2m) of ½" (1.5cm) variegated silk ribbon

6 yds. (5.5m) of ½" (1.5cm) brown rayon seam binding

Medium or heavy wool yarn for ruched frame padding

Locking medium (I recommend a sturdy yarn or cotton twine that matches the fabric strips)

6 15mm brass jump rings

4 pear-shaped crystal beads

2 brass crimp beads

1 brass toggle clasp

6 42" (106.5cm) strands of silk ribbon in varied widths

Self-adhesive fabric

Locker hook

Tapestry needle

Scissors

Pliers

Adhesive

Permanent marker

1 Trace the medium Floral Accent template on page 54 onto canvas three times. Cut out the flowers and secure the edges of each with glue (see Preparing a Shaped Base on page 18). Frame the edges of each piece of canvas with rayon seam binding (see Framing the Base on pages 20–21).

2 Locker hook using the free form method to frame the petals and the center of the design for each flower (see Free Form Locker Hooking on page 27). Fill in the petals working in the spiral method (see Spiral Locker Hooking on page 26).

3 Stitch on the medium or heavy wool yarn to pad the ruched frame area at the center of the flower (see Shaped Ruched Frames on page 29). Cover the padded frame with crushed velvet fabric strips.

4 Sew in the fabric and locking medium tails on each flower (see Sewing in Tails on pages 30–31). You can just clip the ends on the back of each piece instead of sewing them in if you prefer.

5 Use two pairs of pliers to open four jump rings. Place a bead on each jump ring, then close all four jump rings. To arrange the layout of the necklace, gather the silk strips for the chain of the necklace and lay them out on a tabletop as they will drape when worn. Arrange the flowers on top of the silk strips as you want them to appear when the necklace is being worn. Position the beads on jump rings between the flowers. Knot the beads on jump rings to the silk cords.

6 Turn the flowers over and arrange the silk strands over the back of the flowers. Make sure a few of the strands are toward the tops of flowers so they can drape nicely. Line the backs of the flowers with self-adhesive fabric, capturing the silk strands between the flowers and the linings to adhere the flowers to the silk strands (see Self-Adhesive Fabric Lining on page 32). Add a bit of glue around the edge of each piece of lining to attach the flowers to the silk strands more securely.

7 Loop the silk ribbons at one end of the necklace through a brass jump ring. Use pliers and a crimp bead to secure the ribbons to the jump ring. Repeat at the other end of the necklace. Next, use pliers to attach a toggle clasp to the jump rings. Trim the ends of the ribbons diagonally leaving decorative strands of ribbon at each end of the necklace as desired.

Sterling Rose Gift Box

This locker-hooked box is a wonderful example of how you can assemble pieces to create charming three dimensional projects. Made out of cotton, silk remnants and rayon seam binding, it is an inexpensive project that creates a rich and whimsical box. You can inscribe a special message on the inside of the box by embroidering or printing on a piece of fabric. This is a simple design that allows you to create a very special gift.

TECHNIQUES FOR THIS PROJECT

Preparing a Square or Rectangular Base

Spiral Locker Hooking

Sewing in Tails

Assembling Projects

Framing the Base

Embellishing Projects

MATERIALS LIST

5 mesh canvas

40 yds. (36.6m) of ½" (1.5cm) natural muslin fabric strips

20 yds. (18.3m) of ½" (1.5cm) recycled sari silk strips

14 yds. (12.8m) of ½" (1.5cm) fuchsia rayon seam binding

Locking medium (I recommend a sturdy yarn or cotton twine that matches the fabric strips)

2 15mm brass jump rings

Thin cardboard

Self-adhesive fabric

Embellishments such as beads, ribbon, flowers or filigree accents

Locker hook

Tapestry needle

Scissors

Pliers

Permanent adhesive

1 Cut six pieces of canvas: two pieces 26 squares wide and 18 squares tall for the sides of the box, two pieces 36 squares wide and 18 squares tall for the front and back of the box, and two pieces 36 squares wide and 26 squares tall for the top and bottom of the box. Fold over the edges of each piece of canvas by creasing the rows indicated by the gray areas in the patterns on pages 86–87 (see Preparing a Square or Rectangular Base on pages 17–18). Mark the patterns on the canvas pieces if you desire.

2 Locker hook each piece of canvas by following the patterns on pages 86–87 and using the spiral method (see Spiral Locker Hooking on page 26).

3 Sew in the fabric and locking medium tails on each piece of the box (see Sewing in Tails on pages 30–31).

4 Whipstitch the sides of the box to the back of the box (see Assembling Projects on page 33). Whipstitch the front of the box to the sides of the box. Finally, whipstitch the bottom of the box to the front, back and sides of the box.

5 Frame the edges of the top of the box with rayon seam binding (see Framing the Base on pages 20–21). Frame the top edge of the box's front, sides and back as well.

6 Use pliers to open two jump rings. Attach the top of the box to the back of the box using the jump rings as hinges as shown in the photo below.

7 Embellish the box as you desire (see Embellishing Projects on page 34). For the sample shown on page 84, I first glued a filigree accent to the center of the lid of the box, and then glued a flower on top of the filigree piece. I also created a closure for the box by attaching a bead to the front of the box and sewing a beaded ribbon to the lid of the box. When the ribbon is wrapped around the bead on the front of the box, it holds it closed.

8 To make the box sturdy, I suggest reinforcing the sides with cardboard. Cut pieces of cardboard to line the front, back and sides of the box. Wrap each piece of cardboard in self-adhesive fabric, then glue the covered cardboard pieces inside the box.

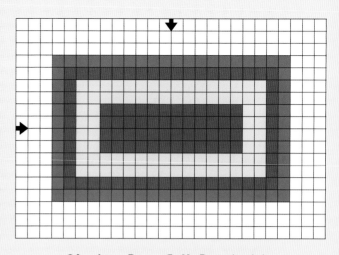

Sterling Rose Gift Box (side)

(project instructions start on page 85)

Sterling Rose Gift Box (top and bottom)

(project instructions start on page 85)

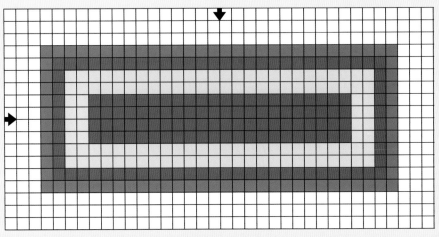

Sterling Rose Gift Box (front and back)

(project instructions start on page 85)

Red Poppy Mat

(project instructions appear on page 89)

Copy at 150% for full-sized template

Red Poppy Mat

This red poppy is a fun and pretty little project that can be used in many ways—hung as wall art or used as a coaster or small trivet. I'm sure you can come up with more ways to use it if you try. It's a great project to start with when you want to go beyond working with squares and rectangles. The design is simple to make as long as you secure your edges. Get creative when you make your own poppy—try adding texture by creating a fringed center.

TECHNIQUES FOR THIS PROJECT

Preparing a Shaped Base

Framing the Base

Spiral Locker Hooking

Free Form Locker Hooking

Sewing in Tails

Self-Adhesive Fabric Lining

MATERIALS LIST

5 mesh canvas

20 yds. (18.3m) of 1/2" (1.5cm) red cotton fabric strips

8 yds. (7.3m) of 1/2" (1.5cm) burgundy cotton fabric strips

5 yds. (4.6m) of 1/2" (1.5cm) charcoal cotton fabric strips

1 1/2 yds. (1.4m) of 1/2" (1.5cm) gold cotton fabric strips

Locking medium (I recommend a sturdy yarn or cotton twine in black, or in a color that matches the fabric strips)

Self-adhesive fabric

Locker hook

Tapestry needle

Scissors

Permanent markers

Permanent adhesive

1 Trace the template on page 87 onto canvas. Cut out the poppy and secure the edges with glue (see Preparing a Shaped Base on page 18).

2 Frame the edges of the canvas with strips of burgundy fabric (see Framing the Base on pages 20–21).

3 Begin locker hooking the pattern, starting at the center of the flower. Work using the spiral method (see Spiral Locker Hooking on page 26).

4 Locker hook using the free form method to frame the petals (see Free Form Locker Hooking on page 27). Fill in the petals working in the spiral method.

5 Sew in the fabric and locking medium tails (see Sewing in Tails on pages 30–31).

6 Line the back of the poppy with self-adhesive fabric (see Self-Adhesive Fabric Lining on page 32).

Be Mine! Heart Ornament

On Valentine's Day, or any day for that matter, what could be sweeter than a handcrafted heart with a special message? You can locker hook this ornament and leave it hanging where it can surprise a loved one, or attach it to a gift-wrapped box. It's fun and easy to make and you can customize it to include your own special message in your favorite colors. This heart ornament is a gift that is sure to be treasured.

TECHNIQUES FOR THIS PROJECT

Preparing a Shaped Base

Framing the Base

Spiral Locker Hooking

Free Form Locker Hooking

Linear Locker Hooking

Sewing in Tails

Self-Adhesive Fabric Lining

MATERIALS LIST

5 mesh canvas

17 yds. (15.5m) of ½" (1.5cm) pink cotton fabric strips

8 yds. (7.3m) of ½" (1.5cm) blue cotton fabric strips

10 yds. (9.1m) of ½" (1.5cm) turquoise recycled sari silk strips

8 yds. (7.3m) of ½" (1.5cm) red flannel fabric strips

Locking medium

16" (40.5cm) piece of red ribbon

Self-adhesive fabric

Turquoise glitter

Locker hook

Tapestry needle

Scissors

Permanent adhesive

Permanent marker

1 Trace the template below onto canvas. Cut out the heart and secure the edges with glue (see Preparing a Shaped Base on page 18).

2 Frame the edges of the canvas with strips of red flannel (see Framing the Base on pages 20–21). You can make a normal frame that covers just the edge of the heart, or you can create a wider frame like I did on this project by whipstitching over two squares at the edge while framing.

3 Locker hook one row around the edge of the heart using pink cotton fabric strips; work in a spiral inside the frame (see Spiral Locker Hooking on page 26). Locker hook a second spiral round with turquoise silk strips.

4 Using the free form method locker hook "be mine" with blue cotton strips (see Free Form Locker Hooking on page 27).

5 Locker hook the background of the design using the linear method; travel locking medium and fabric strips as needed (see Linear Locker Hooking on page 26).

6 Sew in the fabric and locking medium tails (see Sewing in Tails on pages 30–31).

7 Sew a red ribbon through the top center of the heart for hanging. Line the back of the heart with self-adhesive fabric (see Self-Adhesive Fabric Lining on page 32).

8 Use permanent adhesive to trace the letters on the heart. Sprinkle glitter onto the adhesive, then shake off the excess. Let the adhesive dry completely.

Copy at 200% once, then again at 200% for full-sized template

91

CHAPTER THREE

Home Décor

Locker hooking was historically used for making handcrafted rugs for the home. Rugs were primarily made out of wool until locker hookers discovered that strips of fabric could be used as well. You can still make amazing rugs with locker hooking and you can use fabric, wool, yarn or even recycle garments and plastic. You can also use locker hooking techniques with a variety of materials to make many other home décor items like mats, pillows, trivets, wall hangings and even lampshades. In this book I introduce using ceramic or glass tiles to locker hook beautiful trivets or wall hangings. I also introduce one of the smallest and easiest locker-hooked projects, the locker-hooked napkin ring. Whether you're locker hooking a small project or a more complex rug, be sure you try varied materials including some of the leftover fabrics from previous projects. It's such a rewarding feeling to be able to use up beautiful remnants that have collected over the years.

Summer Garden Vine Runner

This table runner incorporates a pretty design in a long format. The floral elements are inspired by red sunflower blossoms with their petals just emerging. The jute twine adds a nice contrast to the wide frame—a look reminiscent of dried vines. This is a project that takes some time to complete, but the finished piece is well worth the effort.

TECHNIQUES FOR THIS PROJECT

Preparing a Square or Rectangular Base

Framing the Base

Spiral Locker Hooking

Free Form Locker Hooking

Linear Locker Hooking

Sewing in Tails

MATERIALS LIST

5 mesh canvas

360 yds. (329.2m) of ½" (1.5cm) pumpkin cotton fabric strips

135 yds. (123.4m) of ½" (1.5cm) brown cotton fabric strips

70 yds. (64m) of ½" (1.5cm) rust cotton fabric strips

65 yds. (59.4m) of ½" (1.5cm) green cotton fabric strips

14 yds. (12.8m) jute twine

Locking medium (I recommend black sturdy yarn or cotton twine)

Locker hook

Tapestry needle

Scissors

Permanent markers

SCALING DOWN

If you love the look of this pattern but don't want to make a project as large as a table runner, you can also locker hook just a portion of this pattern to create something smaller. Try one of the flower elements for a nice mat or trivet.

1 Cut a piece of canvas 248 squares wide and 73 squares tall. Fold over the edges of the canvas by creasing the rows indicated by the gray areas in the pattern on page 96 (see Preparing a Square or Rectangular Base on pages 17-18). Transfer the pattern on page 96 to the canvas.

2 Frame the edges of the canvas with strips of brown fabric (see Framing the Base on pages 20-21). You can make a normal frame that covers just the edge of the mat, or you can create a wider frame like I did on this project by whipstitching over two squares at the edge while framing.

3 Whipstitch over the brown frame with jute twine.

4 Locker hook one row around the edge of the runner using brown fabric strips; work in a spiral inside the frame (see Spiral Locker Hooking on page 26).

5 Locker hook the flowers; start by outlining the exterior and centers in the free form style (see Free Form Locker Hooking on page 27). Fill in the flowers using the linear technique (see Linear Locker Hooking on page 26).

6 Locker hook the swirl and pods design elements using the free form method.

7 Locker hook the background of the design using the linear method; travel locking medium and fabric strips as needed.

8 Sew in the fabric and locking medium tails (see Sewing in Tails on pages 30-31).

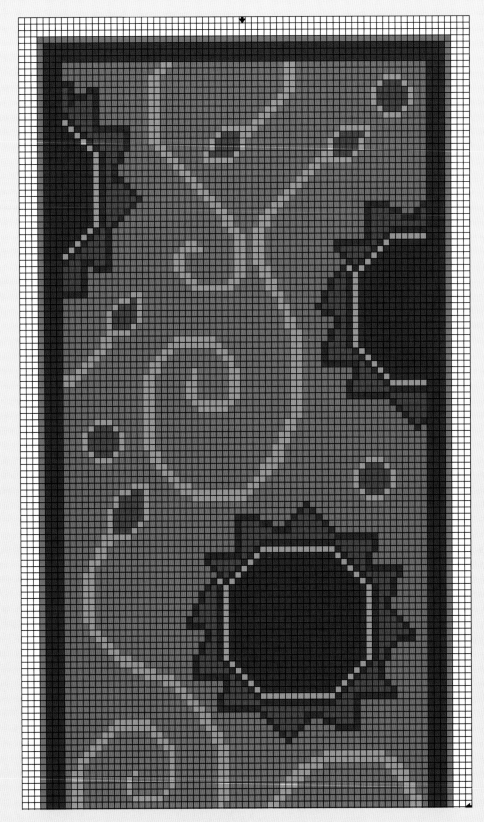

Summer Garden Vine Runner

(project instructions appear on page 95)

This chart shows half of the pattern. To complete the pattern, work from top to bottom, then turn the pattern upside down and work from what is now the top to what is now the bottom.

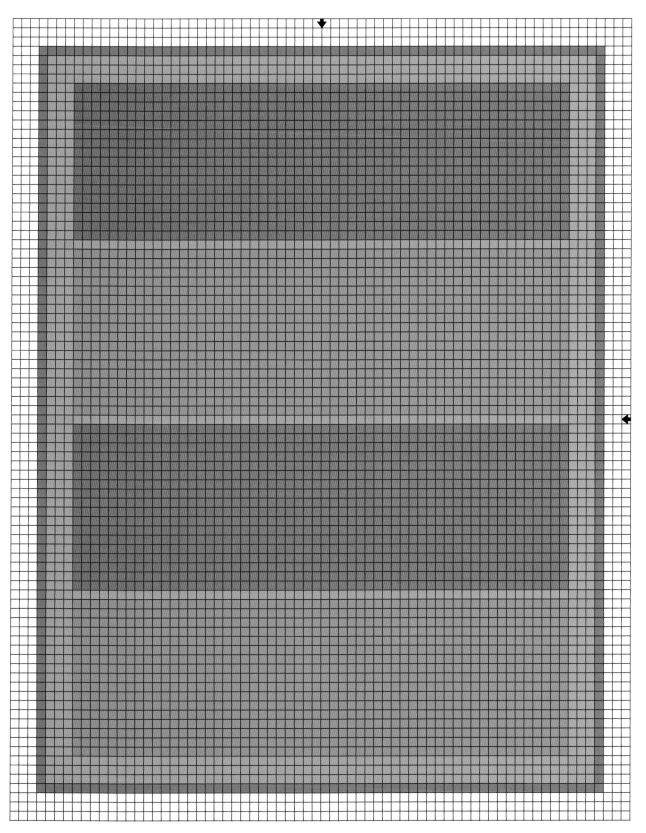

Spring Stripes Placemat

(project instructions appear on page 99)

Spring Stripes Placemat

This simple mat design for spring or summer dining is created with bright, fresh colors. Twine accents set these bright colors apart and add a nice contrast. This is the perfect mat for a casual setting, whether you're planning a luncheon or picnic outdoors. You can coordinate this versatile design with different patterned napkins in similar colors for your place setting. Try customizing a set of mats with your color choices.

TECHNIQUES FOR THIS PROJECT

Preparing a Square or Rectangular Base

Framing the Base

Locker Hooking with Multiple Materials

Spiral Locker Hooking

Linear Locker Hooking

Sewing in Tails

MATERIALS LIST (FOR ONE PLACEMAT)

5 mesh canvas

62 yds. (56.7m) of ½" (1.5cm) fuchsia cotton fabric strips

62 yds. (56.7m) of ½" (1.5cm) orange cotton fabric strips

21 yds. (19.2m) of ½" (1.5cm) green cotton fabric strips

14 yds. (12.8m) jute twine

Locking medium

Locker hook

Tapestry needle

Scissors

1 Cut a piece of canvas 87 squares wide and 70 squares tall. Fold over the edges of the canvas by creasing the rows indicated by the gray areas in the pattern on page 97 (see Preparing a Square or Rectangular Base on pages 17-18).

2 Mark the canvas where the green fabric and twine are used to create frames.

3 Frame the edges of the canvas with green fabric strips (see Framing the Base on pages 20-21). You can make a normal frame that covers just the edge of the mat, or you can create a wider frame like I did on this project by whipstitching over two squares at the edge while framing.

4 Locker hook one row around the edge of the mat using a green fabric strip held together with twine (see Locker Hooking with Multiple Materials on page 24). Work in a spiral inside the frame (see Spiral Locker Hooking on page 26).

5 Locker hook the green dividing lines in the pattern.

6 Using the fuchsia and orange fabric strips, locker hook the rest of the mat in the linear fashion (see Linear Locker Hooking on page 26).

7 Sew in the fabric and locking medium tails (see Sewing in Tails on pages 30-31).

SET YOUR TABLE

Triple or quadruple the length of this placemat to make a matching table runner.

Floral Napkin Ring

This napkin ring easily takes the prize for the smallest and fastest thing you can make from this book. It is such a simple design but can be made to look fun, whimsical or elegant. Try adding beads and fringe to this design for a more creative look. Customize the colors to suit your décor or create multicolored rings with contrasting floral accents for a truly whimsical table setting. I created a set of these for a very charming and warm Thanksgiving table.

TECHNIQUES FOR THIS PROJECT

Preparing a Square or Rectangular Base

Locker Hooking in the Round

Framing the Base

Sewing in Tails

Embellishing Projects

MATERIALS LIST (FOR ONE NAPKIN RING)

5 mesh canvas

14 yds. (12.8m) of ½" (1.5cm) gold cotton fabric strips

3 yds. (2.7m) of ½" (1.5cm) gold rayon seam binding

Locking medium (I recommend a sturdy yarn or cotton twine in black, or in a color that matches the fabric strips)

Silk flower or embellishment of your choice that matches the fabric strips

Locker hook

Tapestry needle

Scissors

Permanent adhesive

1 Cut a piece of canvas 28 squares wide and 13 squares tall. Fold over the edges of the canvas by creasing the rows indicated by the gray areas in the pattern below (see Preparing a Square or Rectangular Base on pages 17-18). Secure the short ends of the canvas with adhesive. Let the glue dry completely.

2 To make the napkin ring you will be working in the round (see Locker Hooking in the Round on page 27). Overlap four squares of canvas to make the canvas piece circular and locker hook the napkin ring following the pattern below.

3 Frame the edges of the napkin ring with rayon seam binding (see Framing the Base on pages 20-21).

4 Sew in the fabric and locking medium tails (see Sewing in Tails on pages 30-31).

5 Attach the silk flower or embellishment of your choice with permanent adhesive (see Embellishing Projects on page 34).

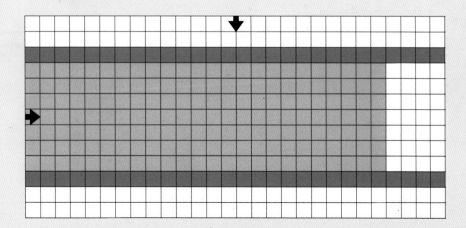

Indigo Dial Trivet

This is an easy-to-make project that results in a piece with contrasting textures. Ceramic tiles make wonderful accents for locker-hooked trivets; not only are they a beautiful embellishment, but they also make the trivet even more heat-resistant. If you include a beautiful tile that you're afraid of breaking, you can use this project as a wall hanging. A collection of these would make stunning wall art in a kitchen or dining room.

TECHNIQUES FOR THIS PROJECT

Preparing a Square or Rectangular Base

Framing the Base

Spiral Locker Hooking

Sewing in Tails

Embellishing Projects

MATERIALS LIST

5 mesh canvas

22 yds. (20.1m) of ½" (1.5cm) indigo cotton fabric strips

12 yds. (11m) of ½" (1.5cm) natural muslin fabric strips

24 yds. (21.9m) of ½" (1.5cm) blue rayon seam binding

Locking medium (I recommend a sturdy yarn or cotton twine that matches the fabric strips)

4" × 4" (10cm × 10cm) ceramic tile

Locker hook

Tapestry needle

Scissors

Permanent adhesive

1. Cut a piece of canvas 52 squares wide and 52 squares tall. Fold over the edges of the canvas by creasing the rows indicated by the gray areas in the pattern below (see Preparing a Square or Rectangular Base on pages 17–18). Transfer the pattern below to the canvas if you desire.

2. Frame the edges of the canvas with blue seam binding (see Framing the Base on pages 20–21).

3. Locker hook the design, starting at the outer edge and working in the spiral method (see Spiral Locker Hooking on page 26). Continue locker hooking inward toward the center, changing fabric as indicated by the pattern. Leave an unhooked area in the center of the trivet for the ceramic tile.

4. Sew in the fabric and locking medium tails (see Sewing in Tails on pages 30–31). Add permanent adhesive to the back of the ceramic tile and place it in the center of the trivet (see Embellishing Projects on page 34). Pull out any loops caught underneath the tile. Let the glue dry completely.

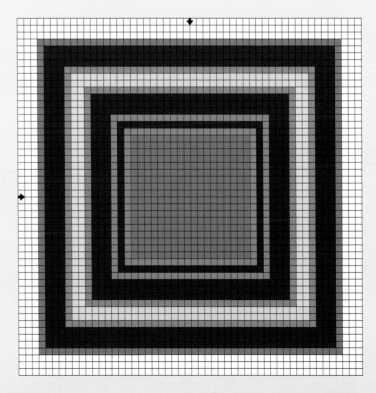

Country French Hamper

Rug canvas isn't sturdy enough to support a large project on its own, but it is possible to create large baskets if you add a little support. In this hamper, bamboo rods provide additional support at each corner. The hamper featured here uses fabric that has a vintage look with a color scheme reflecting the charm of country French décor. It's a unique look with the ruched frames and a puffy frame at the top edge. This basket can be used as a hamper in a nursery or toddler's room or for hand washables. You can also use it as a pretty yarn basket.

TECHNIQUES FOR THIS PROJECT

Preparing a Square or Rectangular Base

Locker Hooking in the Round

Straight Ruched Frames

Spiral Locker Hooking

Sewing in Tails

Assembling Projects

MATERIALS LIST

3.3 mesh canvas

24 yds. (21.9m) of 1¼"–1½" (3cm–4cm) gold and ivory print cotton fabric strips

30 yds. (27.4m) of 1¼"–1½" (3cm–4cm) gold cotton fabric strips

54 yds. (49.4m) of 1¼" (3cm) natural muslin fabric strips

60 yds. (54.9m) of 1½" (4cm) gold cotton lawn or voile fabric strips

38 yds. (34.7m) of 1½" (4cm) steel blue cotton lawn or voile fabric strips

4 2" × 24" (5cm × 61cm) pieces of sheer ivory ribbon

Heavy wool yarn for ruched frame padding

Locking medium (I recommend a sturdy yarn or cotton twine that matches the fabric strips)

4 12" (30.5cm) bamboo rods

Locker hook

Tapestry needle

Scissors

Permanent adhesive

Clamps

1 Cut two pieces of mesh canvas: one piece 47 squares wide and 47 squares tall for the bottom of the basket, and one piece 164 squares wide and 49 squares tall for the basket sides. Fold over the edges of each piece of canvas by creasing the rows indicated by the gray areas in the patterns on pages 106–107 (see Preparing a Square or Rectangular Base on pages 17–18).

2 To make the basket body you will be working in the round (see Locker Hooking in the Round on page 27). Overlap four squares of canvas to make the canvas piece circular and locker hook the basket body following the pattern on page 106. Work from the bottom up. Do not locker hook in the white areas on the chart—the bamboo rods will be placed in these empty spaces.

3 Once you have finished the locker-hooked portions of the basket body, stitch on the heavy wool yarn to pad the ruched frame area of the mat (see Straight Ruched Frames on pages 28–29). Cover the padded frame with strips of cotton lawn or voile fabric strips.

4 To create the puffy frame at the top of the basket, stitch ruched frame padding over the top two rows of canvas. Use a tapestry needle and patterned fabric strips to wrap the top edge of the basket with long loops.

5 Locker hook the bottom of the basket, following the pattern on page 107 and using the spiral technique (see Spiral Locker Hooking on page 26). Once you have finished the locker-hooked portions of the basket bottom, stitch on the heavy wool yarn to pad the ruched frame area. Cover the padded frame with strips of cotton fabric.

6 Sew in the fabric and locking medium tails on the basket bottom and body (see Sewing in Tails on pages 30–31).

7 Align the empty vertical spaces on the basket body with the corners of the basket bottom. Whipstitch the basket body to the bottom of the basket (see Assembling Projects on page 33).

8 Glue the bamboo rods to the basket body at the four corners. Use clamps to hold the rods in place and allow the glue to dry completely.

9 Use a tapestry needle to thread the sheer ribbons through the top edge of the basket at each corner. Tie the ribbons into bows.

CUSTOMIZING THE LOOK

For this design I chose to tear my fabric strips and locker hook with them in a way that would show a little fraying. For your hamper you can choose to do the same, or hide any frayed edges for a cleaner look.

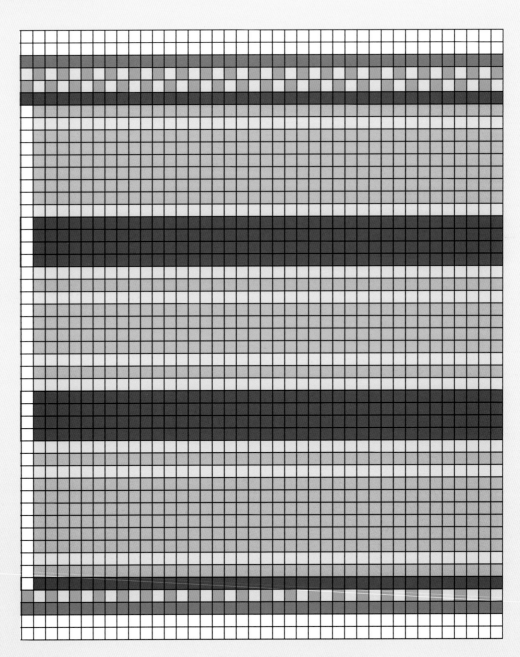

Country French Hamper (body)

(project instructions start on page 105)

(project instructions start on page 105)

This chart shows one quarter of the pattern. To complete the pattern, overlap four squares of canvas to make the canvas round, then repeat the chart above four times, working from left to right.

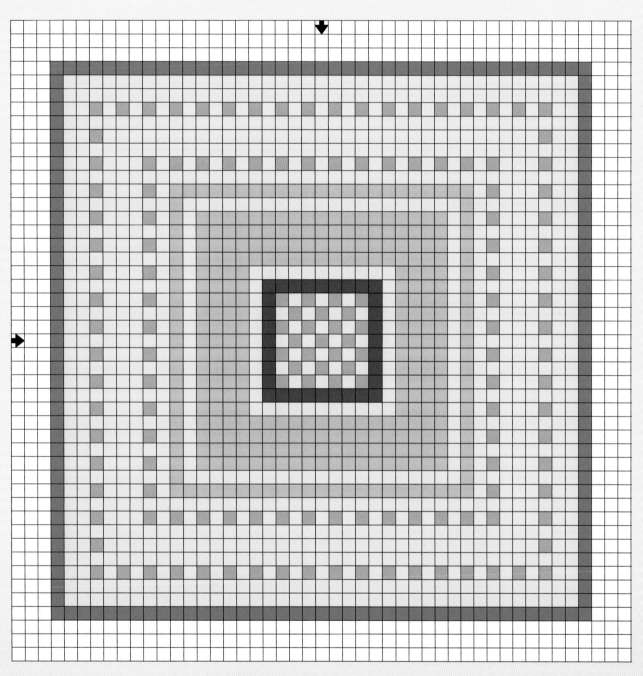

Country French Hamper (bottom)
(project instructions start on page 105)

Striped Mosaic Patio Rug

Sometimes a simple rug design is the best—it works for various areas in a home, including bathrooms. This color combination evokes a tropical or coastal feel. Make this project suit your décor by using other colors or using fabrics you have in your own craft stash.

TECHNIQUES FOR THIS PROJECT

Preparing a Square or Rectangular Base

Framing the Base

Spiral Locker Hooking

Linear Locker Hooking

Sewing in Tails

MATERIALS LIST

3.75 mesh canvas

90 yds. (82.3m) of 1" (2.5cm) blue cotton fabric strips

70 yds. (64m) of 1" (2.5cm) blue/green variegated cotton fabric strips

80 yds. (73.2m) of 1" (2.5cm) gold cotton fabric strips

32 yds. (29.3m) of 1" (2.5cm) ivory cotton fabric strips

16 yds. (14.6m) of ½" (1.5cm) turquoise flannel fabric strips

Locking medium (I recommend a heavy cotton twine or matching heavy cotton yarn)

Locker hook

Tapestry needle

Sewing machine

Sturdy thread

Scissors

1 Cut a piece of canvas 136 squares wide and 97 squares tall. Fold over the edges of the canvas by creasing the rows indicated by the gray areas in the pattern on page 110 (see Preparing a Square or Rectangular Base on pages 17–18).

2 Use a sewing machine with sturdy thread to sew a zigzag stitch to secure the folded edge. Mark the pattern from page 110 onto the canvas if you desire.

3 Frame the edges of the canvas with turquoise flannel (see Framing the Base on pages 20–21). You can make a normal frame that covers just the edge of the rug, or you can create a wider frame like I did on this project by whipstitching over two or more squares at the edge while framing.

4 Locker hook one row around the edge of the rug using a blue strip in a spiral around the frame (see Spiral Locker Hooking on page 26).

5 Locker hook the rest of the rug in the linear method, using cotton fabric strips and switching colors as indicated by the pattern on page 110 (see Linear Locker Hooking on page 26).

6 Sew in the fabric and locking medium tails (see Sewing in Tails on pages 30–31).

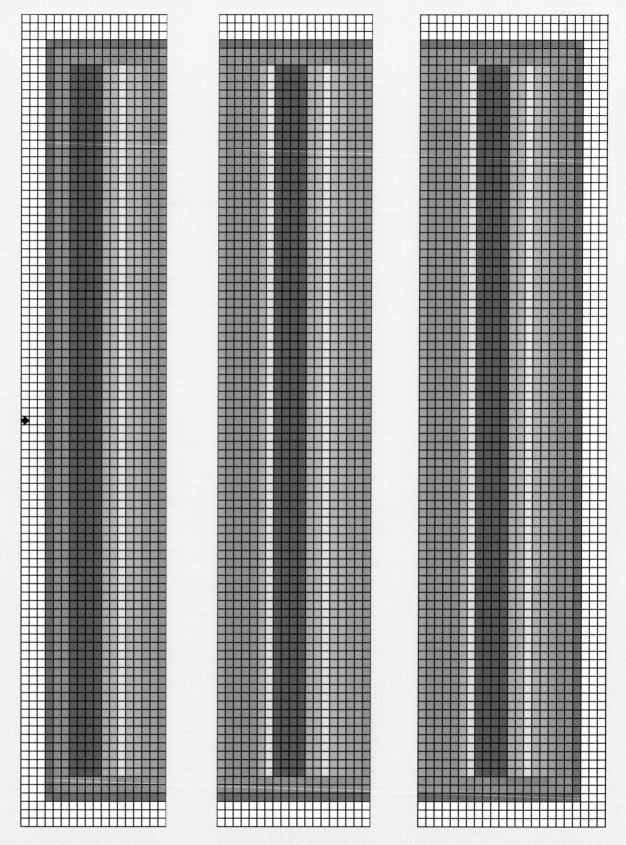

Striped Mosaic Patio Rug

(project instructions appear on page 109)

To complete this rug, work the left pattern once, the middle pattern five times, and the right pattern once.

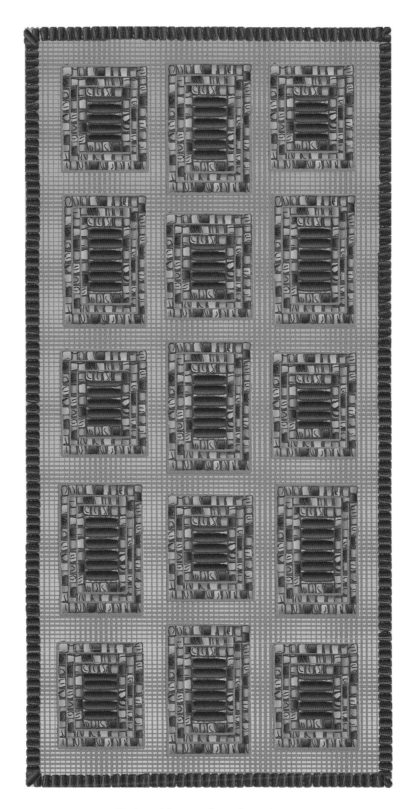

Ruby Stones Lumbar Pillow

(project instructions appear on page 113)

Copy first at 200%, then at 150% for full-sized template

Ruby Stones Lumbar Pillow

Linen burlap is a great fabric to use as a base for locker-hooked pillows, whether you locker hook a complex design to cover the burlap completely or just have minimal coverage like in this simple design. A light brushing of metallic paint provides a touch of glimmer to accent the ribbons and yarns. The same yarns provide a stunning frame with simple stitches. The result is a creative pillow that is remarkably soft to the touch and makes a great accent on a sofa, bed or chaise lounge.

TECHNIQUES FOR THIS PROJECT

Preparing a Square or Rectangular Base

Spiral Locker Hooking

Sewing in Tails

MATERIALS LIST

Linen burlap

60 yds. (54.9m) of ruby ribbon/wool novelty yarn

55 yds. (50.3m) of gray ribbon/wool novelty yarn

Locking medium (I recommend a sturdy yarn or cotton twine in black, or in a color that matches the yarn)

15" × 27" (38cm × 68.5cm) piece of ruby patterned silk satin

12" × 24" (30.5cm × 61cm) pillow form

Metallic paint

Paintbrush

Locker hook

Tapestry needle

Scissors

Sewing needle

Thread

Pins

Steam iron

1 Cut the linen burlap to 15" × 27" (38cm × 68.5cm). Use a steam iron to press under a $1\frac{1}{2}$" (4cm) seam allowance on all sides (see Preparing a Square or Rectangular Base on pages 17–18). The canvas should now measure 12" × 24" (30.5cm × 61cm). Repeat with the ruby patterned silk satin for the back of the pillow.

2 Using a water-based paint that can be ironed to set the color, brush two light coats of metallic paint on the linen burlap. Let each coat dry completely. Make sure the paint goes on in a thin layer. Add a third light coat if necessary to get a metallic sheen. Use an iron to press and set the paint.

3 Using a tapestry needle and ruby ribbon yarn, whipstitch a $\frac{5}{8}$" (1.5cm) frame around the pressed edge of the canvas, leaving the seam allowance out of the stitching.

4 To create the "stones" on the pillow, trace the design on page 111 onto the linen burlap.

5 Locker hook the gray frames around each "stone" using the gray yarn and the spiral method (see Spiral Locker Hooking on page 26).

6 Fill the stones by whipstitching inside the locker-hooked frames with a tapestry needle and ruby ribbon yarn. Sew in the fabric and locking medium tails (see Sewing in Tails on pages 30–31).

7 Pin the locker-hooked linen burlap and fabric backing right sides together.

8 Hand stitch the backing to the locker-hooked canvas on three sides. Insert the pillow form and finish stitching the backing and canvas together.

Bohemian Boudoir Lampshade

When I made this lampshade I was completely inspired by the fabrics. The colors are a study in contrasts—there's the deep pumpkin colored silk, with rich gold and burgundy accents, and the coolness of slate gray in silk crinkle chiffon—a luscious contrast in tones and texture. The silk crinkle chiffon has a nice sweeping drape that works well within the locker-hooked frames. This is a unique locker-hooked design that looks amazing when lit up in a dark room. It's a great accent for a bedroom or near a big upholstered chair.

TECHNIQUES FOR THIS PROJECT

Preparing a Square or Rectangular Base

Locker Hooking in the Round

Linear Locker Hooking

Framing the Base

Sewing in Tails

MATERIALS LIST

3.3 mesh canvas

65 yds. (59.4m) of ³⁄₄"–1" (2cm–2.5cm) recycled sari silk strips in pumpkin, gold and burgundy

30 yds. (27.4m) of 3" (7.5cm) slate gray silk crinkle chiffon strips

9 yds. (8.2m) of ¹⁄₂" (1.5cm) burgundy rayon ribbon

5 yds. (4.6m) of ¹⁄₂" (1.5cm) silk ribbon in pumpkin, gold and burgundy

Locking medium (I recommend a sturdy yarn or cotton twine that matches the fabric strips)

Metallic paint

Paintbrush

Oval lampshade or lampshade frame with a 12" (30.5cm) diameter

Lamp stand

Locker hook

Tapestry needle

Scissors

1. Cut a piece of canvas 122 squares wide and 38 squares tall. Fold over the edges of the canvas by creasing the rows indicated by the gray areas in the pattern on page 116 (see Preparing a Square or Rectangular Base on pages 17–18).

2. Paint the canvas with metallic paint. Allow the paint to dry completely.

3. To locker hook the lampshade you will be working in the round (see Locker Hooking in the Round on page 27). Overlap four squares of canvas to make the canvas piece circular.

4. Locker hook the red portions of the pattern on page 116 using silk strips and the linear method (see Linear Locker Hooking on page 26).

5. Using a tapestry needle and rayon ribbon, frame the top and bottom edges of the canvas (see Framing the Base on pages 20–21).

6. Use a tapestry needle and silk crinkle chiffon strips to create the draped portions of the lampshade. Stitch through the canvas along the sides of each locker-hooked rectangle, through every other square in the same locker-hooked row as the silk. The photo below shows the pattern of stitches you'll need to make when you're draping the chiffon. Fill each rectangle with nicely draped strips.

7 Sew in all of the tails except the ones at the base of the shade (see Sewing in Tails on pages 30-31). You can leave the fabric tails at the bottom of the lampshade and they will become part of the fringe.

8 Tie silk ribbons to the bottom of the shade to create fringe that is 1½"-2" (4cm-5cm). Trim the strips of fringe on the diagonal.

9 Slip the locker-hooked piece over the base lampshade and attach it to the lamp base.

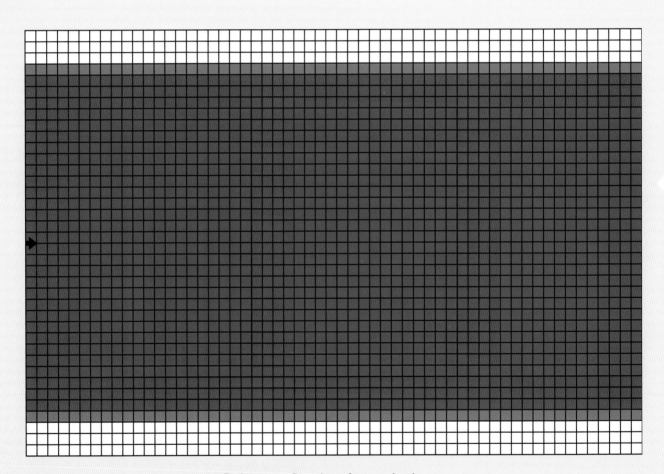

Bohemian Boudoir Lampshade

(project instructions start on page 115)

This chart shows one half of the pattern. To complete the pattern, overlap four squares of canvas to make the canvas round, then work the chart from left to right twice.

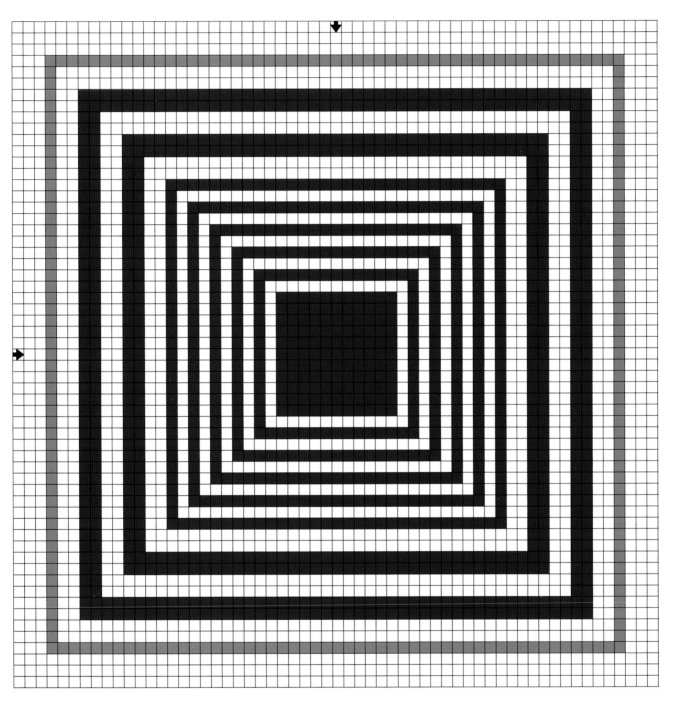

Spiral Squares Rug

(project instructions appear on page 119)

Spiral Squares Rug

When I started experimenting with the idea of recycling denim I created the first spiral square for this design. It's a simple design that is infused with great texture from the frayed osnaburg strips and denim accents. Once I made the first square, I liked it so much I decided to make more to create a rug. This textured beauty looks amazing against a wood or tiled floor. Try it at the foot of your bed or in a bathroom.

TECHNIQUES FOR THIS PROJECT

Preparing a Square or Rectangular Base

Spiral Locker Hooking

Sewing in Tails

Assembling Projects

Framing the Base

MATERIALS LIST (FOR ONE SQUARE)

3.75 mesh canvas

13 yds. (11.9m) of ½"–¾" (1.5cm–2cm) denim fabric strips

42 yds. (38.4m) of ½" (1.5cm) osnaburg fabric strips

30 yds. (27.4m) of ½" (1.5cm) blue flannel fabric strips, plus additional yardarge for assembly and framing

Locking medium

Locker hook

Tapestry needle

Scissors

1 Cut a piece of canvas 59 squares wide and 59 squares tall. Fold over the edges of the canvas by creasing the rows indicated by the gray areas in the pattern on page 117 (see Preparing a Square or Rectangular Base on pages 17–18). Transfer the pattern on page 117 to the canvas if you desire.

2 Locker hook the design, starting at the center with flannel and working in the spiral method (see Spiral Locker Hooking on page 26). Continue locker hooking outward toward the edge of the square, changing fabric as indicated by the pattern.

3 Sew in the fabric and locking medium tails (see Sewing in Tails on pages 30–31).

4 Repeat Steps 1–3 to create as many squares as you desire.

5 Whipstitch the squares together using strips of blue flannel (see Assembling Projects on page 33).

6 Frame the edges of the rug with flannel (see Framing the Base on pages 20–21).

7 Sew in any remaining tails.

SUBSTITUTING STRIPS

If you choose to use quilting weight cotton for this design, increase the width of the strips to ¾"–1" (2cm–2.5cm).

Summer Poppy Mat

The design for this mat is reminiscent of a quilt design. You can use it as-is, or make more squares and assemble them for a table runner or even a rug. The ruched frame technique adds a special frame-within-a-frame look, but you can also choose to just locker hook the ruched frame area if you like. The color scheme is a warm Mediterranean look but can be customized to match your own décor.

TECHNIQUES FOR THIS PROJECT

Preparing a Square or Rectangular Base

Framing the Base

Spiral Locker Hooking

Free Form Locker Hooking

Straight Ruched Frames

Sewing in Tails

MATERIALS LIST

5 mesh canvas

90 yds. (82.3m) of ½" (1.5cm) rust cotton fabric strips

60 yds. (54.9m) of ½" (1.5cm) gold cotton fabric strips

29 yds. (26.5m) of ½" (1.5cm) blue cotton fabric strips

88 yds. (80.5m) of ½" (1.5cm) ivory cotton fabric strips

10 yds. (9.1m) of ½" (1.5cm) blue rayon ribbon

24 yds. (21.9m) heavy wool yarn

Locking medium

Locker hook

Tapestry needle

Scissors

1 Cut a piece of canvas 80 squares wide and 80 squares tall. Fold over the edges of the canvas by creasing the rows indicated by the gray areas in the pattern on page 122 (see Preparing a Square or Rectangular Base on pages 17–18). Transfer the pattern on page 122 to the canvas if you desire.

2 Frame the edges of the canvas with blue ribbon (see Framing the Base on pages 20–21).

3 Begin locker hooking the pattern, starting at the outer edge to create the frames. Work using the spiral method (see Spiral Locker Hooking on page 26).

4 Locker hook the center of the flower using the spiral method, then work in the free form method to frame the petals (see Free Form Locker Hooking on page 27). Fill in the petals working in the spiral method.

5 Stitch on the heavy wool yarn to pad the ruched frame areas of the mat (see Straight Ruched Frames on pages 28–29). Cover the padded frame with strips of cotton fabric.

6 Sew in the fabric and locking medium tails (see Sewing in Tails on pages 30–31).

CUSTOMIZE AND COMBINE

Combine elements of the Summer Poppy Mat with the Indigo Dial Trivet on page 102 to create a unique design of your own. In this example I used the outer ruched frame of the Summer Poppy Mat with the spiral design and tile of the Indigo Dial Trivet.

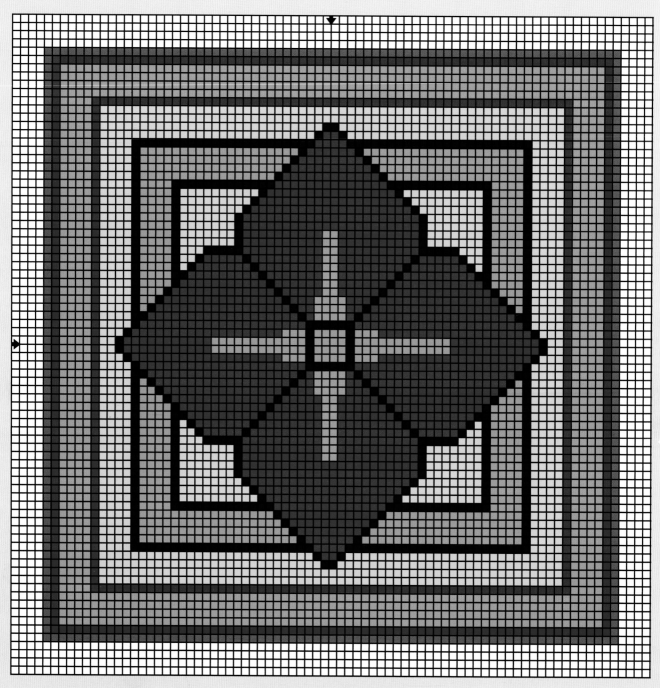

Summer Poppy Mat
(project instructions appear on page 121)

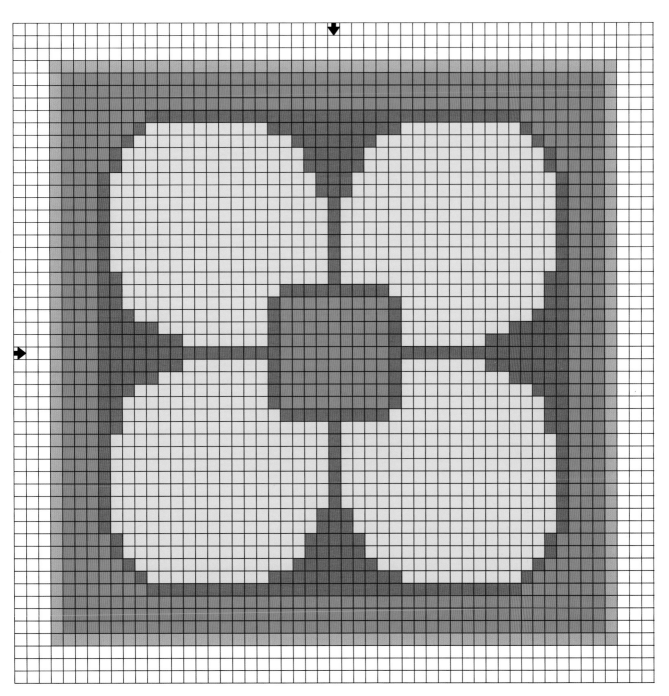

Petals Pillow

(project instructions appear on page 125)

Petals Pillow

Every toddler's bed deserves a small, cozy pillow to mingle with stuffed animals. This design is perfectly suited for that. However, it's also a lovely accent pillow on larger beds. Create this pillow in soft pastels or fun color combinations to add a whimsical touch to your décor.

TECHNIQUES FOR THIS PROJECT

Preparing a Square or Rectangular Base

Spiral Locker Hooking

Free Form Locker Hooking

Linear Locker Hooking

MATERIALS LIST

5 mesh canvas

80 yds. (73.2m) of ivory bulky yarn

80 yds. (73.2m) of caramel bulky yarn

16 yds. (14.6m) of 1/2" (1.5cm) wide raspberry rayon ribbon

Locking medium

1 1/4 yds. (1.1m) ivory pom-pom trim

10" × 10" (25.5cm × 25.5cm) piece of osnaburg fabric

9" × 9" (23cm × 23cm) pillow form

Locker hook

Tapestry needle

Scissors

Sewing needle

Thread

Steam iron

1 Cut a piece of canvas 53 squares wide and 53 squares tall. Fold over the edges of the canvas by creasing the rows indicated by the gray areas in the pattern on page 123 (see Preparing a Square or Rectangular Base on pages 17–18). Transfer the pattern on page 123 to the canvas if you desire.

2 Begin locker hooking the pattern, starting at the center of the flower and using caramel yarn and the spiral method (see Spiral Locker Hooking on page 26).

3 Using the free form method, locker hook the outline of the center and petals with rayon ribbon (see Free Form Locker Hooking on page 27).

4 Locker hook the petals with ivory yarn. Start by outlining each petal with a single row of locker hooking, then fill in the petals by working in the linear method (see Linear Locker Hooking on page 26).

5 Locker hook the rest of the pillow in the spiral method with caramel yarn.

6 Steam press a 1/2" (1.5cm) seam allowance on each edge of the osnaburg backing.

7 Hand stitch the osnaburg to the locker-hooked canvas on three sides with the edge of the pompom fringe sandwiched between them. Insert the pillow form and finish stitching the osnaburg, trim and canvas together.

Resources

Check your local craft supply retailer for these or similar supplies, or call the manufacturer directly to find a supplier near you.

CANVAS

Lacis
www.lacis.com

M.C.G. Textiles
www.mcgtextiles.com

TOOLS

Lacis
www.lacis.com

YARN

Berlini Italian Knitting Yarns
www.numei.com/berliniyarn.htm

Berroco
www.berroco.com

Crystal Palace Yarns
www.straw.com

Lantern Moon
www.lanternmoon.com

Lion Brand Yarn
www.lionbrand.com

Louisa Harding
www.louisaharding.co.uk

Patons
www.patonsyarns.com

Tahki Stacy Charles, Inc.
www.tahkistacycharles.com

Trendsetter Yarns
www.trendsetteryarns.com

FABRIC

Bali Fabrics Inc./Princess Mirah Designs
www.bali-fabrics.com

Hoffman Fabrics
www.hoffmanfabrics.com

Robert Kaufman
www.robertkaufman.com

RIBBON

Hanah Silk
www.hanahsilk.com

Mary Jo Hiney Designs
www.maryjohineydesigns.com

May Arts
www.mayarts.com

EMBELLISHMENTS

Art Glitter
www.artglitter.com

Nina Designs
www.ninadesigns.com

Prima Marketing Inc.
www.primamarketinginc.com

Rupert, Gibbon & Spider, makers of Jacquard Products
www.jacquardproducts.com

Vintaj Natural Brass Co.
www.vintaj.com

LAMPSHADES & FRAMES

The Lamp Shop
www.lampshop.com

Index

Lock in some more crafting fun!

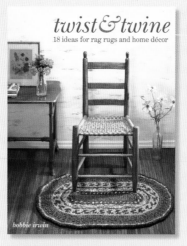

HOOK, LOOP & LOCK
Create Fun and Easy Locker Hooked Projects
Theresa Pulido

Hook, Loop & Lock features over 25 fun projects that turn yarn and strips of fabric into rugs, handbags, wall art, jewelry and more! Perfect for locker hooking beginners and all crafting enthusiasts.

TWIST & TWINE
18 Ideas for Rag Rugs and Home
Bobbie Irwin

Twist & Twine will introduce you to the basic techniques of fabric twining with projects such as rugs, placemats, table runners and napking rings. This book also includes a chapter on building looms.

VINTAGE CROCHET FOR YOUR HOME
Best-Loved Patterns for Afghans, Rugs and More from 1920-1959
Coats & Clark

Inside Vintage Crochet for Your Home you'll find classic styles and projects from the Coats & Clark archives in a variety of difficulty levels. There are 30 projects packed with vintage charm, including shopping bags, potholders, placemats, afghans and more. Each project has been remade using modern yarns and colors, and each pattern has been rewritten for the modern crocheter. Make some of yesterday's patterns for today's home!

❖ These and other fine Krause Publication titles are available at your local craft retailer, bookstore or online supplier, or visit our website at www.mycraftivitystore.com.

Follow us on Facebook for all of the latest in craft news and new books from F+W Media Crafts: facebook.com/fwcraft